PATTERNS OF INDIAN THOUGHT

In the same series
John B Chethimattam, *Consciousness and Reality*

INDIAN RELIGIONS AND PHILOSOPHIES

PATTERNS OF INDIAN THOUGHT

A Students' Introduction

JOHN B CHETHIMATTAM

GEOFFREY CHAPMAN
LONDON DUBLIN MELBOURNE 1971

Geoffrey Chapman Ltd
18 High Street, Wimbledon, London SW19
Geoffrey Chapman (Ireland) Ltd
5–7 Main Street, Blackrock, Co. Dublin

This edition, first published 1971
© 1971, John B Chethimattam
ISBN 0 225 66001 6

This book is set in 10 on 12pt. Baskerville

Made and printed in Great Britain by
A. Wheaton & Co., Exeter, Devon

CONTENTS

Abbreviations used in the footnotes

Upanishads:—

Ait Up	Aitareya Upanishad
Brih Up	Bṛhadâranyaka Upanishad
Chând Up	Chândogya Upanishad
Isa Up	Isavasya (Isa) Upanishad
Kath Up	Katha Upanishad
Kau Up	Kauṣitaki Upanishad
Ken Up	Kena Upanishad
Mait Up	Maitrâyaṇi (Maitri) Upanishad
Mândy Up	Mândûkya Upanishad
Mûnd Up	Mûndaka Upanishad
Pras Up	Praśna Upanishad
Svet Up	Svetasvatara Upanishad
Tait Up	Taittîriya Upanishad

Sûtras:—

Bad S	Badarâyama Sûtras
Br S	Brahma Sûtras
Ny S	Nyâya Sûtras
Vai S	Vaiśeṣika Sûtras
Ved S	Vedânta Sûtras
Yog S	Yoga Sûtras

Bhâṣyas:—

G Bh	*Śankara's Gîta Bhâṣya*
Sank Bh	Śankara's Bhâṣya
	(e.g. Ved S Sank Bh = Śankara's Bhâṣya on the Vedânta Sûtras; Tait Up Sank Bh = Śankara's Bhâṣya on the Taittîriyopanishad; etc.)
Sri Bh	Râmânuja's Śrî Bhâṣya

Miscellaneous:—

AV	Atharva Veda
BG	Bhagavad Gîta
Mândy K	Mândûkya Kârikâ
RV	Ṛg Veda
Sâm K	Sâmkhya Kârikâ
Vedârth	Vedârtha Saṁgraha
VP	Vishṇu Púrâṇa

PREFACE

'Christians, Jews, Buddhists, Hindus, Muslims and others are all faced today (for the first time) by a joint challenge : to collaborate in building a common world,' said Dr. Wilfred Cantwell Smith in his inaugural Convocation Address as Director of the Centre for the Study of World Religions of the Harvard University. This modern challenge is something which India faced all through her millennia-old history. India is a world in miniature. In her long history, all the major world cultures, philosophies and religions met together, interacted and converged to form a single tradition.

Hence, the story of this long dialogue in Indian tradition has a message for the contemporary world : only in an intimate inter-action or transaction can a real dialogue take place. Information gathered by scientific study may create an academic interest in other traditions. Only an interpretation as if from within the tradi-tions, by a sort of empathy through contact with persons belonging to the respective traditions, will provide an insight into the inner dynamism of the faith behind the traditions. Only when the con-vergence of these various approaches to man and his life's problems is taken into account will a true dialogue emerge. To keep up the dialogue, the identity and uniqueness of each tradition also have to be kept intact. With regard to India, this authentic dialogue among the various cultural traditions, philosophical thought-patterns and world religions is a historical fact.

The scope of this short study is to provide a sort of introduction to the millennia-long dialogue in the Indian sub-continent. This limited scope restricts the study to generalities, leaving further details to more specific works.

My intention here is to show that no single tradition can claim a monopoly of truth, and none can pretend to be a perennial philo-sophy all by itself. Each tradition has its own particular mode of approach, its own specific problems to handle and peculiar solutions

vii

to propose. All these become meaningful only in complementarity with other traditions.

I must warn the reader about two important omissions. The Dravidian religio-cultural tradition was left out because it needs a whole book in order to bring out its subtle but radical influence on the Indian tradition. Similarly, the highly significant Zoroastrian or Parsi tradition is not discussed here, because its specific influence on Indian life is not quite evident.

The material presented here has been already discussed in courses given by me to several groups in India, and at the Fordham University, New York. I am particularly grateful to my students who, by their discussions, helped me to clarify several points and also indicated what they expected in an introductory book of this nature.

BANGALORE   JOHN B CHETHIMATTAM, c.m.i.
NEW YORK   *Dharmaram College*
1 May 1970   *Fordham University*

CHAPTER I

INDIA IN THE CONTEXT OF HISTORY

The Confluence of Religious Cultures

'At the dawn of history India started on her unending quest, and trackless centuries are filled with her striving and the grandeur of her success and her failures,' said Pandit Jawaharlal Nehru, the first Prime Minister of Independent India, in his famous speech, 'A Tryst with Destiny', delivered in the Constituent Assembly on 14 August, 1947, the eve of India's independence. In her long history, India never claimed to be a great political potentate, nor had she ever any extensive empire outside her confines, like China, Rome or Britain. In fact, she had a sad past of long foreign dominations, punctuated only by short periods of freedom. Very rarely was she unified and remained united as a single kingdom. On the other hand, this in no way diminished her influence on world history, since her political conquerors were often deeply influenced by her spiritual insights and carried the lessons they learned from her far beyond her geographical limits.

Jambudveepa, the land of the *jambu* (pear) fruit, a name also justified by India's geographical shape, is marked out from the rest of the world by a long boundary of oceans and mountains. The northern barrier of the Himalayan and Hindukush mountains protects her from the cold winds blowing from the north through Siberia. The Arabian, Indian, and Bengal seas form her western, southern and eastern boundaries. But these natural barriers never isolated her. From the earliest memories of history, wave after wave of invaders, settlers and traders found their way into India over desolate mountain passes and through stormy seas. The Aryan settlers who entered India around 2000 B.C. called the great river on the border *Sindhu,* ocean, and the Persians, according to their wont, converted the initial 's' into an aspirate and coined the term *Hindu.* The river came to be known as Indus, the land as Hindustan and the people Hindus.

1

The Indian population consists of a great variety of races and tribes. Several races and tribes were already settled in India when the Aryans made their entry. Even the Aryans were not a single race, but themselves consisted of or were accompanied by several tribes and races. They were followed down the centuries by Persians (Pactys = Pathans, Sakas = Marathas, Yuech = Kushans—521–485 B.C.), Greeks (327–325 B.C.), Huns (A.D. 454), Arabs (A.D. 712), Munghols (1230), Turks (1398) and later by the Portuguese (1498), French (1664), and the British (1639), all of whom sought their fortune in India, and opened trade routes through which India in turn spread her commerce, culture and especially religions to China, Burma, Cambodia, Java and the whole of South-East Asia.

India is a land of variety. It is geographically divided into three regions: North India, Deccan, and South India. North India is bounded on the north by the Himalayan and Hindukush mountains, on the south by the Vindhya mountains, and covers the Indo-Gangetic plain. Deccan, which means the southern country, is the region extending from the Narmada river in the north to the Godavari and Krishna rivers in the south, a plateau held up, as it were, by two mountain ranges, the Eastern and Western Ghats. The southern end and the two coasts constitute South India. This geographic stratification creates a climatic diversity, ideal ground for a variety of cultural patterns and especially for a multitude of tongues, though all are held together by a long and consistent tradition. Every trader and settler, invader and conqueror left his progeny in India along with his own contribution to its cultural past.

India of today living her past

When in 1946, the British, after a century of uneasy imperial rule, sought to redeem the pledge they had given through the two world wars to grant independence to India, they found that they had to decide the fate of nine directly ruled British provinces and over six hundred native states, so far held together only by the military might of the British Empire. For a long time they had pleaded the impossibility of giving independence to this motley crowd as to a single nation. They argued that the Hindu and Muslim communities could never co-exist peacefully in a single republic: 'Neither of the two communities are actually indigenous in the country, as both the Hindus and Mohammedans originally came as conquerors from without; yet both have been settled in the country long enough to be regarded as its native population,' wrote Lytton, Governor of Bengal, in 1929.[1] Katherine Mayo wrote her *Mother India*, which went into forty-two printings within a decade and detailed all the weaknesses, miseries, superstitions, and abominations of India; at least for self-protection against these evils of India, the cultured West had a right to keep it under the benevolent control of the British Raj.[2] Several Indian and European writers tried to answer her charges and pointed out the power of endurance of 'Father India',[3] though for all that, it was an 'Unhappy India',[4] for, 'no curse is greater than that of political subjection to another people'.[5]

The plan of the British Cabinet Mission that visited India to decide her independence was to leave her as a loose federation of three groups of states : one containing those provinces with a Hindu majority; the second, those with a Muslim majority; the third, the crowd of independent native states. This plan, reluctantly accepted in the beginning by the Indian leaders, was subsequently rejected by them. The Muslim agitation under Mohommedali Jinnah for a separate state for the Muslims ended up in the formation of Pakistan, formed from the North-Western Frontier Province, and the Muslim-majority halves of Bengal and Punjab. The rest of the country became independent India at midnight on 15 August, 1947. The six hundred and eighteen native princes were forced by persuasion and popular agitation to accede to the Indian Union. India proclaimed herself a Republic on 26 January, 1950. This

---

[1] Victor Alexander George Robert Lytton, 'Hindu Muslim Unity', *India*, ed. D. R. Bhandarkar (Calcutta, 1929), pp. 175–80.

[2] Katherine Mayo, *Mother India* (New York: Blue Ribbon Books, 1927): 42nd printing, October 1937, p. 409: 'India has carried the principles of egocentricity and of a materialism called spirituality to a further and wider conclusion than has the West. The results, in the individual, the family and the race, are only the more noteworthy, for they cast a spotlight toward the end of that road.'

[3] C. S. Ranga Iyer, *Father India, A Reply to 'Mother India'* (London: Selwyn and Blount, 1927, reprinted nine times in 1927); Ernest Wood, *An Englishman defends Mother India. A Complete Constructive Reply to 'Mother India'* (Madras: Ganesh & Co., 1929); Syam Sunder Chakravarty, *My Mother's Picture (An attempt to get the Hindu Spirit in connection with the Mayo Challenge)*, (Calcutta); Dhan Gopal Mukerji, *A Son of Mother India Answers* (New York: E. P. Dutton & Co., 1928); K. Natarajan, *Miss Mayo's Mother India, A Rejoinder* (Madras: G. A. Natesan & Co., 1927).

[4] Lal Pat Rai, *Unhappy India* (Calcutta, 1928).

[5] *Ibid.*, p. ix.

independent India does not have the grandeur of Rome, nor the splendour of Egypt, nor even the greatness of the mighty empires of Persia and China. Yet it is unique in a special way, a wonder of religious culture and social history.

The wonder of India is the continuity of her civilization and the unity of her culture. As Will Durant has eloquently expressed it,[6] she forms 'an impressive continuity of development and civilization from Mohenjodaro, 2900 B.C. or earlier, to Gandhi, Raman and Tagore'. In her, every form of faith, from popular idolatry to subtle mysticism, and a thousand forms of philosophy with a continuity stretching over millennia, are arrayed. She has kept up a scientific tradition which started with the astronomy of three thousand years ago and continues with the Nobel Prize-winning scholars of our day. She has a democratic tradition of an untraceable antiquity lost in the village panchayats of old. In epic poetry, painting, architecture and other art forms, India has an unparalleled tradition extending from pre-history to modern times.

Some Western writers have tried to emphasize the diversity of India in clime and culture, race and tongue, and declared that the unity of India is a fiction—at best, a political expediency and, at worst, the imposition of priestly myth and superstition on an unsuspecting people.[7] But the history of India is not a dead past, nor its unity a mere fiction. No nation is made up of amorphous masses. Each one grows according to sociological laws into an organized community with living traditions and reasonable expectations for the future. India's unity is the product of her long history by the integration into her life-stream of all the cultural elements that flowed into her, Dravidian and Aryan, Greek and Munghol, Turk and Pathan alike.

India's strength

This in no way suggests that India is a paradise of unity and harmony. The struggle for independence was accompanied by bitter communal conflicts leading to the massacre of thousands. Independence, which was marked by the division of the Bengal and Punjab provinces, witnessed the most cruel blood-bath. The formation of

---

[6] Will Durant, *Our Oriental Heritage*, The Story of Civilization, Vol. I (New York: Simon & Schuster, 1954), p. 391.

[7] Cf. e.g., Ronald Segal, *The Anguish of India* (New York: Stein & Day, 1965), pp. 19–27.

the Republic of India with a progressive Constitution in no way healed the chronic ills of over-population and widespread poverty. Even the most enthusiastic leaders of the independence struggle had no illusions. As Pandit Nehru candidly declared, to take this great mass of people from the 'cowdung economy' (a term suggesting the Indian village custom of using dried cowdung for fuel) to the industrial economy of the modern developed nations is not an easy task. Even to feed a population more than two-and-a-half times that of the United States of America from an arable land only one-third that of the U.S.A. will be a difficult proposition with any amount of planning. The material wealth of India that attracted all traders, fortune-seekers and invaders into the Asian sub-continent is now definitely a matter of the past. Poverty has come to be an inseparable companion of her religious culture.

Even culture can be a problem. As Nehru wrote in his *Glimpses of World History,* composed during his long prison years, poetry and culture are often 'a rich man's game played with the lives of the people'. When a culture goes on singing the glories of its past, and, throwing aside all originality, merely imitates past productions, it is nearing its death. When little is done to relieve the suffering of the people as a whole, it is 'the evening of a civilization'.[8]

On the other hand, this point should not be exaggerated to mean that to be fed and to be overfed is more important than all religious and cultural values.[9] Important as the economic and political problems are, they are not the most basic ones in the life of a nation. An affluent society with no ideals to live up to can end up in debauchery. Comforts of life can be a trap unless they have a meaningful life to support. India has found her strength, not in wealth or political power, but in man himself, his growth in society. Pandit Nehru, speaking to a Muslim University group a few months after independence, said: 'India's strength has been twofold; her own innate culture which flowered through the ages, and her capacity to draw from other sources and thus add to her own.'[10] She is too strong to be swept away by outside currents and too wise and alert to be isolated from the outside world.

There were several other factors that contributed to the continuity

[8] Cf. *Nehru on World History*, condensed by Saul K. Padover (New York: Day Co., 1960), pp. xii and 46–7.

[9] Cf. Ronald Segal, *op. cit.*

[10] Speech at Aligarh Muslim Univ., Jan. 24, 1948.

of India's culture. Her social unity was a hierarchical one into which every race that came in was integrated and assigned its proper place and status, its religion taken into a definite place in the comprehensive Hindu cult, and its cultural contributions assigned a proper meaning. Even Christians and, in certain cases, Muslims also, accommodated themeselves to this religious social structure.

Another secret of this millenia-old social stability is that honour, prestige and influence are ascribed to learning and sanctity, and not to power and wealth, which always had to take second place. The Brahmin, the scholar and the sage were always respected all over India. These consciously nourish and control the cultural unity and create the greater culture from which the so-called little cultures, or the particular traditions of regions, sections and villages, draw their inspiration and meaning. These are the people least influenced by opportunism and rarely carried away by the passing fashions of the day.

A third basis for the cultural unity of India is its closeness to and identification with Nature. Extending from the thirty-seventh parallel in the north to the eighth parallel in the south, with a medley of mountains, valleys, plateaux and deserts, India has all the diversity of nature that presents a macrocosmic mirror to man's own nature. Hence, Indians invoked the Mother Earth and spoke of their country as 'Mother Land'. For them, all the rivers are sacred; the cow is sacred, the Banyan Tree and several other trees are sacred. *Tirthas,* or sacred places of pilgrimage, are scattered all over India, from the snowclad Bhadrinath in the north down to Kanyakumari at the southern tip. These helped the devotee to conceive India as a single sacred phenomenon. The ancient stories of *Ramayana* and *Mahabharata,* though located in the north, are so representative of Indian life that they are considered the common past by all, and are sung at popular festivities.

As Vincent A. Smith has stated in his introduction to *The Oxford History of India,* India has a fundamental unity not produced by mere geographical isolation or political control, but one transcending 'the innumerable diversities of blood, colour, language, dress, manners and sect'.[11]

Sri Aurobindo Ghosh, one of India's early freedom fighters, wrote in 1918 that India's special creativity has to be in the line

[11] Oxford, 1967.

of an intellectual approach to spiritual realization. This is a fourth reason for her cultural stability. He says: 'One thing seems at any rate certain, that the spiritual motive will be in the future of India, as in her past, the real originative and dominating strain.'[12] According to him, the sudden change to modernization, undergone by Japan in recent times, can never happen to India. 'India lives centrally in the spirit . . . with a less ready adaptiveness of creation, but a greater, intenser, more brooding depth.' On account of this reflective and introspective bent of mind, her steps have to be deliberate and procedures hesitant till the readjustment comes from the profoundest inwardness.[13]

As there is a diversity of men, so also there is a diversity of cultures. Each one has to contribute to the world community according to its own proper genius. The existence of reflective and introspective types of personality serves to turn the attention of more active and efficient persons to their conscious selves in the midst of the busiest and engrossing preoccupations. In the same way, India's cultural tradition may be called, in a certain sense, the conscience of humanity. In it, several distant and divergent cultures have, by historical accident, met together and flowed together to form in the course of centuries a single tradition, a single culture. Synthesis and tolerance are the outstanding characteristics of this tradition, and this harmonizing function may be India's contribution towards the formation of a world culture.

[12] *The Renaissance in India* (Calcutta: Arya Publishing House, 3rd ed., 1946), pp. 44–6.
[13] *Ibid.*, p. 34.

CHAPTER II

INDUS VALLEY RELIGIOUS CULTURE

There were people living in India long before the Aryans entered India. Not to mention the paleolithic people who left their crude stone instruments behind them in the Soan villages of North India, and the more polished stone instruments in the Mysore region in South India in the inter-glacial period between 400,000 and 200,000 B.C., the excavations of the Harappa and Mohenjodaro sites in the earlier part of this century have revealed the existence of a prosperous population in the Indus Valley in the 4th and 3rd millennia B.C. It had a well-developed culture and was a pioneer of civilization along with Babylon, Assyria, Sumer, Akkad and Egypt.[1]

In that remote age, the Indus Valley people had well-planned cities with well-arranged streets, from nine to thirty-four feet wide, intersecting at right angles and dividing the cities into square or rectangular blocks, very good water supplies and ingeniously engineered drainage systems. Their civilization built comfortable houses with expensive burned brick and stone, made good pottery, painted with pleasant patterns, and even knew the use of metal, as can be concluded from the few copper implements discovered at the excavation sites. The large granary at Harappa and the spacious bath at Mohenjodaro are unique constructions in comparison with other contemporary civilizations. The people of the Indus Valley had various household articles made of pottery, stone, shell, faience, ivory, copper and bronze.[2]

It was a widely-spread culture, extending roughly 950 miles north-south, and it remained steady and stable for well over a thousand years. Hence, scholars conclude that it was not a culture based on 'the secular instability of the court', but rather on 'the

[1] Stephen Fuchs, *The Origin of Man and his Culture* (Bombay: Asia Publishing House, 1963), pp. 47–9.

[2] *The Vedic Age*, The History and Culture of the Indian People, Vol. I, ed. R. C. Majumdar and A. D. Pusalker (Bombay: Bharatiya Vidya Bhavan, 1957), pp. 169–98.

unchanging traditions of the temple'.[3] The religion that inspired that culture was very close to nature, of the type practised by other early agricultural communities of antiquity. The people of the Indus Valley were in close contact with their contemporaries in other parts of the world. From the finds at the sites of Harappa and Mohenjodaro, it is evident that these places were in communication, not only with different distant parts of India like Rajasthan, South India and Kashmir, but also with distant countries like Afghanistan and the islands of the Persian Gulf. Besides this, their intercourse with Mesopotamia is established by the fragments of vases made of Indian 'potstone' discovered at Al-Ubaid, and by the identification of trefoil patterns with those of certain Sumerian 'Bulls of Heaven'.[4]

However, in the matter of religion, in contrast to the contemporaries of Mesopotamia, one thing is fairly evident about the people of the Indus Valley : they had no temples or shrines or anything of the sort. If they had any, so far no trace of those distinct holy places has come down to us. They had a concrete experience of the universe and did not feel the need to draw sharp contrasts between spirit and matter, sacred and profane, purely good and purely evil and the rest of the pairs that constituted the beginning of metaphysics in the West. Perhaps, in sharp distinction from the threatening natural conditions of the Middle East, nature was benign and plentiful in the Indus Valley. Hence, the gods of the Indus Valley displayed on seals and seal-rings are shown in perfect friendship with nature.

Directness and concretivity were common features of primitive religion. Only very meagre data are available concerning the religious expressions of the Indus Valley people, and therefore conclusions have to be cautiously drawn, tallying the findings of the sites of Harappa and Mohenjodaro with the more plentiful sources concerning the religious cultures of Sumer, Assyria, Babylon, Akkad and Egypt.[5] For the whole Mesopotamian world, sea and land, river and earth represented the gods. The Euphrates-Tigris rivers rendered the land fertile. People did not know to whom to

[3] A. L. Basham, *The Wonder that was India* (London: Sidgwick & Jackson, 1961), pp. 10–24.
[4] *The Cultural Heritage of India*, Vol. I (Calcutta, 1958), pp. 111–3, 126.
[5] Cf. W. F. Albright, *Archaeology and Religion of Israel* (Baltimore, 1956), pp. 44–54; *From the Stone Age to Christianity* (New York: Doubleday, Anchor Book, 2nd ed., 1957), pp. 146–99.

ascribe the paternity in the process. The river and the sea were powerful and productive, but they were also the maternal receptacle of life-force. Hence, Tiamat and Enlil (the Lord of the storm) sometimes appear as androgynous gods and sometimes as goddesses aligned with different husbands, but mainly the earth, Ea. They were not only procreative forces for a good number of things but often, through flood and tide, destructive monsters as well. Ea, the earth, could withstand the onslaught of the waters, but the river could retaliate by drying up in summer, leaving the earth barren. Then An, the Sumerian god of heaven (Re', the Egyptian Sungod), as father and mediator, came to settle their quarrels. Man had not mastered these primitive elements nor understood their working sufficiently to deal with them as mere things. He did not care much for abstract thinking about distinguishing between a pure Absolute beyond and the concrete material universe.

One of the most primitive phenomena of religion is the fertility cult, in which one approaches the divine for more children and more food. Even at the Aurignacian age, we come across stone, bone, and ivory reliefs and statuettes of nude women, stressing only breasts, abdomen, navel and pubic region. They indicate women in advanced pregnancy.[6] These often represented imitative cults in which, by representing natural creative processes, man attempted to accelerate them. Fertility cults are also the most outstanding feature of the Indus Valley region. The figure of the Mother Goddess predominates. The pregnant female figure and the figure of the Mother suckling the child are frequent expressions of a faith in a maternal principle in nature. Figurines akin to the Great Mother of the Indus Valley have been found in large numbers from Iran to the Aegean, especially in Elam, Mesopotamia, Transcaspia, Asia Minor, Syria, Palestine and Egypt, and even in the islands of Cyprus and Crete.

Along with representative cults, mythology or sacred story-telling should also have evolved. Max Müller has said that 'mythology is a disease of language'. Though this is not fully correct, primitive language was, however, undoubtedly more complex and elaborate than modern languages derived from it, because of its mythological expressions in which a great deal of symbolism occurred. Primitive man did not indulge in logical and philosophical abstractions, yet he showed an extraordinary power for pre-logical abstraction and

---

[6] *From the Stone Age to Christianity, op. cit.,* p. 132.

expressed general qualities such as goodness, truth, purity and others. So also, proto-metaphysical conceptions like totem, holiness, abomination, *mana*, divine, etc., were easily understood and expressed.

Mythology is basically the sacred story, narrating the irruption of a divine power into human existence. Here, the outstanding concept is that of power, the *mana, orenda* and *wakonda* of ethnologists. As Rudolf Otto has characterized it, it is both *tremendum* and *fascinans,* fearsome and at the same time attractive. Man feels insecure in life and is afraid of the after-life. At the same time, he feels a spontaneous optimism and a confidence in a force beyond. The male divinities of the Indus Valley religion are shown with a horned headdress, which was the symbol of supernatural power.

Power finds expression in human religiosity in different ways. As the Epic of Gilgamesh, a story widespread in the whole Middle East in the second millennium B.C., sets forth, man feels power first in his own brute force, then in the dangers threatening him from the outside, thirdly, in the divinely preferred help, and finally, in the inevitability of death. Hence, sex, procreation, drunken dance, and the rest, are primary symbols of this force. The male deities of the Indus Valley are all nudes. The bronze statue of the dancing figure found among the deposits was most probably a religious object.

However, the experience of suffering and death and the presence of enemies brings man to an awareness of a threatening power. This force is inevitable and overpowering. There is, at first, an attempt to conquer it and bring it under control through magical means. In primitive religions where sacrificial ritual is emphasized, it often degenerates and assumes the aspect of feeding the gods, who are assumed to wait for their meal like hungry animals, or even of bribing the gods to attain the sacrificer's wishes.

Nevertheless, the inevitability of tragedies like death and the irresistibility of calamities like flood make man find hope only in total reliance on a power beyond. The deluge myth, which one finds in the Gilgamesh epic, in the Bible, and in ancient Hindu mythology, show man's spontaneous and universal faith in the miraculous intervention of the gods.

The Indus Valley religion also presents another approach to power, namely, that of asceticism. The horned god with an erect phallus, surrounded by the animals and dancing figures, is shown in a yogic posture. The external symbols of power converge on man, and man himself is centred in himself, concentrating his attention on his authentic and ultimate ground, his own self. Here, power is interiorized.

Thus, in the Indus Valley, the basic tone of Indian religiosity is already set : a concrete experience of nature, a positive approach to sex and fertility, and an approach to power and salvation through interiority.

CHAPTER III

THE SPIRIT OF THE VEDAS

Indian tradition is the synthesis of the various religious cultures that came to India one after another in the course of centuries. The Vedas, the earliest literature of humanity that has come down to us, can be called the basic outline of this synthesis. First composed as hymns to be sung in common, memorized and handed down by hearing, later compiled into *samhitas*, or collections, according to particular needs—especially liturgical—and finally fixed as sacred tradition, these books present the fluid thought of a nomadic people slowly moving into the Indo-Gangetic plain.

This literature is quite remarkable both in quantity and in the depth of its message. It is also significant with regard to the continuity and consistency of the tradition. According to William D. Whitney, 'no other nation has placed in our hands so ample a literary representation of an equally distant epoch of its mental development'.[1] According to him, in spite of the fact that the Indian people lacked a sense of history and cared little to preserve historical records, 'their text exists in a state of almost absolute purity, offering hardly a corruption or variant reading to perplex their modern student'.[2] The reason for this stability may be that, with the transition from the spontaneous natural expression of religious feeling to a formal and organized religion, the Vedic books came to be looked upon as an 'indispensable part of worship, its only efficient medium' and in some manner identified with religion itself.

Concept of God

The Vedic people worshipped many gods, principally representing natural phenomena, just like the Greeks and other Indo-European races. They also had a sacrificial rite, according to which offerings

---

[1] William D. Whitney, 'On the History of the Vedic Texts', *Journal of the American Oriental Society,* Vol. IV (1854), pp. 247–61.
[2] *Ibid.,* p. 247.

were made to the gods in fire. Fire was the consumer of the sacrifice, a messenger between gods and men, and also one of the important gods. The *Rig Veda* begins with a hymn to Agni, the god of fire : 'I praise Agni, the chosen priest, god, minister of sacrifice. . . . Worthy is Agni to be praised by the living as by ancient seers.'[3] The *Rig Veda* speaks of thirty-three gods.[4] The chief among them are Mitra and Varuna, Agni and Vayu (air), Aryaman, Aditi, Maruts, Savitar, Brahmanaspati,[5] Pushan,[6] Ushas[7] and Rudra.[8] Of these, Varuna is mentioned as the king of heaven, who knows everything and governs everything.[9] Rudra is sometimes a title of fire,[10] but at other times a separate god, gentle and beneficient, refulgent as bright gold, the best among the gods.[11] The individuality of the gods is not very much emphasized. Hence, in some hymns one god may appear supreme, and in others another deity will be presented as the lord of all. Light is an important feature of the gods. Varuna, Indra, Savitar, Ushas and Agni are all presented as gods of light. In several places it would appear that Pushan, Savitar, Tvastar, etc., are merely different names of the Sungod. There are sufficient traces in the Vedas of the ancient Sun worship of the Aryan people. The ancient god Bhaga still lingers as a source from which functions of the different gods are derived.[12]

Another indication of the earlier relationship of the Aryans with other races is the mention of Asuras (Assyrian—Ahura) as gods. Tvastar, the principal among them, is presented as the gods' artisan, entrusted with the task of making thunderbolts for Indra. Ribhus are the disciples of Tvastar.[13]

Metaphysical thought

What distinguishes the Vedic people from the earlier races of the Indus Valley and those of Mesopotamia is the former's capacity for abstract thought. The Vedas express the idea of the beyond,

[3] *RV*, I, 1.
[4] *RV*, I, 45, 2.
[5] *RV*, I, 40, 1.
[6] *RV*, I, 42.
[7] *RV*, I, 48.
[8] *RV*, I, 43, 5.
[9] *RV*, I, 25.
[10] *RV*, I, 27, 10.
[11] *RV*, I, 43, 5.
[12] *RV*, I, 95; 136, 2.
[13] *RV*, I, 20, 6; 110, 3; 151, 4.

not only in anthropomorphic conceptions of gods, but also in real metaphysical terms. Thus, the idea of the infinite is one of the first positive metaphysical steps. For the early Greek thinkers, infinite was imperfect. But for the Vedic people, infiniteness was the necessary characteristic of the perfect and absolute. Goddess Aditi is seen as the infinite maternal principle, the visible form of the infinite :

Aditi is the heaven, Aditi is mid-air, Aditi is the Mother and the Sire and the Son.
Aditi is all gods, Aditi five-classed men, Aditi all that hath been born and shall be born.[14]

God Vishnu, who makes his entry as a minor deity, is soon acclaimed as 'the Ancient and the Last (*purvâya vedhase naviyase*)' and as 'the primeval germ of Order (*ritasya garbham*) even from his birth'.[15] Instead of particularizing heaven and earth as individual gods, as in Assyrian and Babylonian mythology, the *Rig Veda* presents them as cosmic principles.[16]

The Vedic poet fixes his attention on the Sun, the yearling calf, with seven brothers and seven sisters, coursing on his one-wheeled chariot, and asks the sages to tell him, 'how the boneless One supports the bony?', namely, how the unsubstantial, subtle, maternal principle can support this substantial, visible, material universe.[17] The answer is equally mysterious as the question :

They told me these were males, though truly females; he who hath eyes sees this, the blind discerns not.
The son who is a sage hath comprehended : who knows this rightly is his father's father.[18]

This is probably a piece of grammatical mysticism : *rasmi*, the ray of the Sun, though personified as feminine is a masculine noun. The rays are the father of the crops on earth. So the Sun is the father's father. The son who is a sage, instructing his ignorant father, is his father's father. So is one who understands the mystery of the cosmos ! The mystical flight of the poet is particularly apparent in the following verse :

Where those fine birds hymn ceaselessly their portion of life eternal, and the sacred synods,

[14] *RV*, I, 89,10.
[15] *RV*, I, 156.
[16] *RV*, I, 159.
[17] *RV*, I, 164, 4.
[18] *RV*, I, 164, 16.

There is the Universe's mighty Keeper (*visvasya bhuvanasya gopah*), who wise (*dhîrah*) hath entered into me the simple.[19]

His metaphysics is a combination of cosmic experience as well as of ritual worship. He sees how the cosmic tree of beings is paralleled and completed by the internal formation of the *Gâyatri*[20] and of the sacrificial hymn. He finally reaches the comprehensive view : 'Dyaus is my Father, my begetter . . . this great earth is my kin and Mother. . . . This altar is the earth's extremist limit, this sacrifice of ours is the world's centre.'[21] He does not understand his own being. He only knows that he is a portion of the cosmic unity, of which speech is a first expression.[22]

The dominant feature of the Vedas is this unending quest for the ultimate meaning of life and of the world. Of the four Vedas, *Yajur* and *Sama* are strictly liturgical in character, while *Rig Veda* and *Atharva Veda* consist of heterogeneous material, and are historical and theoretical in their approach. All the common theories concerning the origin of the universe and of man, of moral code and social organization, are found in the thought of those early invaders of India : the world came out of sacrifice; it was built by the gods; it came out of a primeval golden seed, *hiranyagarbha*, a cosmic egg which split into two forming earth and heaven. These theories are indifferently and indiscriminately stated.

There is also a certain attempt at synthesis of the various theories. Thus the *Purusha Sukta,* the Hymn of the Primeval Person, weaves all these different theories into a single myth, and places the Person at the centre and head of everything : he is all, at the beginning of all, and from him is everything else, including the castes and classes of people, and scripture itself : 'The Purusha is this all, that which was and which shall be.'[23] From the initial chaos of 'non-existence' he, the one existence, by himself generated all.[24]

This Purusha-centred world view was to become India's special way of looking at reality. It emphasizes the interiority of the spirit, the Atman, the self of man, as the focal point of all reality. Around

[19] *RV*, I, 164, 21.
[20] *Gâyatri* is the sacred prayer, said to be the Mother of the Vedas, revealed to Sage Visvamitra: 'Let us meditate upon the excellent glory of the God Savitar; may he inspire our minds' (*RV*, III, 62, 10).
[21] *RV*, 164, 33, 35.
[22] *RV*, I, 164, 37.
[23] *RV*, X, 90.
[24] *RV*, X, 82; 129.

this centre there revolve concentric circles of interpretation which are, on the one hand, personalistic and even anthropomorphic and, on the other, impersonal and theoretical. Thus, the Person is identified with Varuna, the Supreme Lord, who creates all and reads the minds of all men. This all-knowing Lord 'propped up the heavens and measured out the expanse of earth; all worlds did the great king take into his possession'.[25] He discriminates men's truth and falsehood.[26] 'If two persons sit together and scheme, King Varuna is there as a third, and knows it.'[27] Each of the other gods, too, has his special assignment. Prajapati creates; Agni presides over sacrifice; Indra regulates thunder and rain; Vishnu guides men on their paths. They are also presented in pairs : Agni and Vishnu come together for sacrifice and ritual;[28] Mitra and Varuna are together protectors of the cosmic order;[29] Vayu and Savitar provide light and air.[30]

Rita

On the other hand, there is, in all this speculation, a strong undercurrent of emphasis on the underlying impersonal values, symbolized by food, speech, life (breath), and above all *rita*, which may be translated as cosmic order, law, truth or reality. This is an awareness of the mystery of reality. *Atharva Veda* speaks of *rita* as the 'highest secret, where everything becomes of one form', 'the immortal', three-quarters of which are 'deposited in secret', 'the first-born of righteousness (*rita*) abiding in beings as speech in the speaker'.[31] Mitra, Varuna and Aryaman are the guardians of the moral order. They provide happiness to those who keep *rita*.[32] Knowledge of *rita* destroys sins. The foundations of *rita* are firm. On it stand earth and heaven.[33]

Speech

Similarly, ultimate importance is given to speech. It is a symbol of the basic and subtle aspect of reality. Certain Vedic hymns on

[25] *RV*, VIII, 42, 1.
[26] *RV*, VII, 49.
[27] *AV*, IV, 16.
[28] *AV*, VII, 29, 30.
[29] *AV*, IV, 29.
[30] *AV*, IV, 25.
[31] *AV*, II, 1.
[32] *RV*, I, 90, 91.
[33] *RV*, IV, 23.

speech read like the self-declaration of Wisdom in the sapiential books of the Bible :

> I go about with the Rudras, Vasus, Adityas, all gods; I bear Mitra and Varuna, Indra and Agni. I am queen of all good things; enjoyable of gods and men, source of life and knowledge. I stretch the bow for Rudra. . . . I myself blow forth like the wind, taking hold upon all beings, beyond the sky.[34]

Brahman

The Vedic quest is for the ultimate reality. The word designating the Supreme Reality originally meant speech, what is spoken, the magical word. Then it was shifted to indicate the one gifted with magical power, and finally came to be reserved to mean the ultimate hidden reality. Being the ultimate ground and support of all, 'Brahman is food'.[35] He is the initial being, the one without a second, the sole reality from which everything takes origin.[36]

The *Atharva Veda* speaks of Brahman thus :

> The Brahman that was first born of old . . . he enclosed the fundamental nearest shapes of it, the womb of the existent and of the non-existent.
> He who is soul-giving, strength-giving; of whom all, of whom even the gods wait upon the instruction. . . .
> He who by his greatness became sole king of the breathing, winking animal creation; of whom immortality, of whom death is the shadow. . . . He by whom the heaven and earth are extended and fixed, he who maintains the greatness of the snowy mountain.[37]

This Brahman is *bhûman*, the fullness of all things. He envelops all things. All things are in him and he in all things.

This concept of Brahman became the synthesis of both the impersonal and personal outlook on reality. Even though the Aryans recognized a multitude of gods, they all became unified in Brahman, as his forms and functions. All worship came to be centred in sacrifice consumed by fire. This Brahman was also the culminating point of the philosophical thought of India in its attempt to define reality; Brahman is the supreme reality, infinite being, pure consciousness, beside whom there is no other.

[34] *AV*, IV, 30.
[35] *Tait Up*, III, 1.
[36] *Chând Up*, VI, i, 4.
[37] *AV*, IV, 1.

CHAPTER IV

THE FORMATION OF INDIAN RELIGIOUS CULTURE

Aryan–Pre-Aryan Religious Interaction

When, towards the middle of the second millennium B.C., the Aryan tribes emerged into the broad plains of the Indus, the refined men of Harappa and Mohenjodaro were ill-prepared to face them. The nomadic Aryans were physically stronger than the sedentary people of the Indus Valley. They had discovered iron and used iron weapons and also had horses, which their adversaries lacked. These physically superior invaders looked down upon the lazy, dark-skinned, flat-nosed townspeople, easily defeated them, and occupied the country. It is understandable that the vanquished were made captives or pushed out of the territory to the north into Kashmir, to the east into the Bengal-Orissa region and to the south into the Deccan. Their millennium-old civilization was destroyed. The Aryans found a particular pleasure in razing to the ground the strong fortresses and cities ingeniously built by the former settlers. Indra, the war god of the Aryans, is often called *Puramdara*, destroyer of cities. Still, a portion of the pre-Aryans should have managed to stay behind, either accepting the absolute dominion of the newcomers or entering into some kind of a compromise with them. In any case, it was only natural that the culture of the newcomers should influence the older one, and in turn be also modified. This proceeded according to the laws of social interaction. Naturally, the conquering foreigner assumed a certain superiority for his cultural values and looked upon the conquered as uncultured. Hence, there was a first moment of foreign domination, which the victor used to impose his own values and customs and even religion on the vanquished.

Aryanization

In several hymns of the *Rig Veda*, the theme is the struggle between the *Aryas* and *Dasas*. *Arya* means noble and *Dasa* means slave. Whether these are terms coined by the newcomers in the enthusiasm of their victory, or whether they had some relation with their original tribe names, is not easy to determine. The term *Arya* has a close relation to the agricultural occupation of the people on account of its spurious derivation from the Latin *arare*, to plough. There were conflicts not only between Aryans and the pre-Aryan Dasyus, but also among Aryan tribes themselves. Thus, one reads in *Reg Veda* : 'Both these our foes, our Dasa and our Arya enemies, hast thou, heroic Indra, destroyed.'[1] 'Ye smote and slew the Dasa and Arya enemies and protected Sudas with your succour, O Indra-Varuna.'[2] There is even the complaint that Indra slew Aruna and Chitraratha, who were in fact allies of the Aryans.[3]

Aryan did not constitute a religious designation. The Aryans practised the Manu cult for religion. Manu was supposed to be the first person who kindled the sacrificial fire and instituted ceremonial worship. There are several references to the Manu cult in the *Rig Veda*.

Agni, together with the gods and the children of Manush, celebrating a multiform sacrifice with hymns.[4]

To the Manus who spread the grass (*i.e.*, who sacrifice) may he (Agni) grant shelter.[5]

. . . when these pious Manus, sacrificing and spreading the sacrificial grass, offer thee (Agni) oblation. . . .[6]

The *Rig Veda* praises the gods 'who made the Manus superior to the Dasas' and extols Indra for having in a hundred ways 'preserved the Arya worshipper . . . and subjected the dusky skin to the Manus.'[7] The Manu cult was centred in sacrificial rites performed in fire, which symbolized all the gods.

To all appearances, Aryans imposed their religion and culture on the non-Aryans to a great extent. The former cults persisted

[1] *RV*, VI, 33, 3.
[2] *RV*, VII, 83, 1.
[3] *RV*, IV, 30, 18; II, 12, 4.
[4] *RV*, V, 2, 12.
[5] *RV*, X, 91, 9.
[6] *RV*, VI, 21, 11.
[7] *RV*, I, 130, 8.

on the local level in remote villages. But they were brought under the supervision of the Brahmins and in some way were put in relation with the Manu worship. Native languages were slowly replaced by Sanskrit, or radically transformed by Sanskritization. Only in the southern part, the Deccan, which could not be conquered by the Aryans, could the pre-Aryan Dravidians withstand the Aryanization process and preserve the individuality of their tradition, maintaining the Dravidian languages, which already had a well-evolved literature, independent of Sanskrit influence. Later, the Sanskrit influence affected them, too; but it was by way of healthy assimilation which left their identity intact. Even today, the Dravidian village worship can be distinguished from the Hindu cult, though in the long run, these village gods also had to submit to the Brahmanical sovereignty.

Non-Aryan contribution

However, at the very time the Aryans imposed their culture on the conquered people of India, they were also silently assuming a good many elements from the religion and culture of the Indus Valley people. The non-Aryans had a down-to-earth, living religious tradition and the Aryans, with their abstract form of worship, consisting principally of hymns and fire offerings, were very much impressed by its freshness and concreteness. The whole epic culture presented in the *Mahabharata* and *Ramayana* shows signs of a fusion between the two traditions.

Here, the contrast and complementarity between the Aryan and Babylonian or Chaldean religious outlooks may be relevant. Scholars suggest that the pre-Aryan Dâsas or Dasyus were also settlers in India, belonging originally to the Dahae of the Caspian steppes, and culturally related to the Chaldeans and Mongolians. According to the French scholar Lenormant, the Aryans worshipped the good and beneficent deities in nature, while the Mongolians and Chaldeans tried to propitiate the malevolent spirits.[8] The former emphasized the qualities of the spirit, goodness, truth, beauty, and loved abstract systems of thought. Their gods were models of nobility, ideals for men to imitate. They looked on the body with a certain contempt, and were ashamed of sex and all its manifestations. On the other hand, the Chaldeo-Mongolians emphasized the

---

[8] Cf. Bal Gangadhar Tilak, 'Chaldean and Indian Vedas', *R. G. Bhandarkar Commemoration Volume*, pp. 32ff.

qualities of the body, strength and courage; they loved the open-air life. Sex and passion were sacred for them, and fertility cults formed a prominent part of their religious worship. They cared little for systems of abstract thought, and treasured their concrete experience as the most important.

The encounter between Aryans and Dasyus brought the two cultural approaches and religious attitudes face to face. There are clear evidences of a fusion between the two in the Hindu culture that evolved in the Indo-Gangetic plain. As Bal Gangadhar Tilak points out, the *Atharva Veda*, V, 13, in the *mantra against snake* poison, contains a clear reference to the Chaldean Tiamat myth, *asitasya taimatasya . . . urgulasya duhita*, the androgynous dragon, the primeval monster of the nether world, by killing which Marduk brought order out of chaos and created humanity.[9] The Tiamat-Marduk fight has its counterpart in the Ahi (Vritra)–Indra fight of the Vedas. Indra is called Vritrahan, Apsujit, the killer of Vritra and conqueror of Apsu.[10] Apsu is the husband of Tiamat, the Abyss, or the primeval chaos in the Babylonian myth.[11] Indra is also called *saptahan*, killer of the seven-headed,[12] and Tiamat is sometimes represented as having seven heads. There are several other terms in the Vedas which show an affinity between the different traditions, like *Yahu, Yahvi, Yahvati* (similar to the Chaldean and Hebrew *Yahweh*), *asura* (Chaldean *ahura*) and others.[13]

Eka Vratya and Siva

The evolution of the Siva cult in Hinduism may be taken as a clear case of the fusion of the Aryan and non-Aryan traditions. In the Vedas, there is no mention of a Siva cult. Rudra,[14] later identified with Siva, is shown as a beneficent deity, the best among the gods. But, in the *Atharva Veda,* Book XV, which is known as the *Vratyasukta*, we read of a certain Vratya, who influenced Prajapati and became *Mahadeva*, a great god, and finally made the gods his footmen and became the *Eka Vratya*, the supreme

[9] Cf. Bal Gangadhar Tilak, *op. cit.*, pp. 32ff.
[10] *RV*, VIII, 4, 4, 2.
[11] *The Ancient Near East, An Anthology of Texts and Pictures*, ed. James B. Pritchard (Princeton University Press, 1958), pp. 31–9.
[12] *RV*, X, 49, 8.
[13] D. R. Bhandarkar, *Some Aspects of Indian Ancient Culture,* Sir William Meyer Lectures, 1938–9 (Madras University, 1940), pp. 30–6.
[14] *RV*, I, 43; V, 5; I, 27, 10.

deity. He is said to have taken to himself Indra's bow, assumed *sraddha,* or faith, as *pumschali,* or mistress, Mitra as a bard, and discernment (*vijnânam*) for a garment. He wore day for his head-dress (*ushnîsham*), and special ear-rings, and adorned himself with *kalmali,* the special jewel.[15] Bhava, Sarva, Pasupati, Ugra, Rudra, Mahadeva and Isana are said to be, in ascending order, earlier stages or manifestations of Eka Vratya or his attendants.[16] The deity, revelling in drinking and dancing in the company of harlots, presents the model of a non-Aryan character. He is made here the starting point of a cosmic meditation. Eka Vratya very much resembles the Mohenjodaro deity with horns and a tall headdress, shown as Pasupati, the god of animals. The bronze statue of the dancing girl excavated at Mohenjodaro is clearly a religious figure, the *pumschali* of the god. Sexual symbolism is prominent : the deity is shown, like the Siva idols, with an erect phallus.

Both the Indus Valley horned god and the Atharvan Eka Vratya may be taken as the prototypes of the post-Vedic Siva, noted for a formidable bow. He is fond of *sura,* or intoxicating drink, dances his *tandava* along with drunken imps, and wears a headdress, and is also called *ushnîshin* (one who wears a headdress). Like the Mohenjodaro deity and Vratya, Siva is said to be a great ascetic, but at the same time is depicted with an erect phallus. Siva combines in himself different aspects of Mahadeva, Rudra, and Pasupati. Thus, in the Siva cult, the Aryan and pre-Aryan religious traditions strike a compromise.

Vishnu and Indra

Religious history also undergoes change on account of the internal conflicts of a society. When the nomadic and pastoral Aryans settled in the Indo-Gangetic plain and some of them took to agriculture, their gods and forms of cult also had to be modified. God Indra is a typical case. He is clearly a late-comer in the Vedic pantheon. Though he is said to be one of the seven Adityas in *Rig Veda,* X, 72, in the list of the Adityas in *Rig Veda,* II, 27, 1, there are only six Adityas and Indra is not one of them. The early Aryan gods were Dyaus or Dyava (Jupiter), Prithvi, Mitra, Varuna, Amsa, Bhaga, Aryaman and Daksha. Brahmanaspati, probably replacing

---

[15] *AV,* XV, 1 and 2.

[16] *AV,* XV, 5. For a detailed discussion of the Vratya problem and for all the different solutions proposed, cf. A. C. Banerjea, *Studies in the Brahmanas* (Delhi: Motilal Banarsidass, 1963), pp. 81–172.

Dyaus, became the creator of all gods, including Indra.[17] Indra is
said to be the god of rain, but he is not the god of the gentle rain
that shepherds liked, but the god of thunderstorms and torrential
monsoon rains on which the farmers depended for bumper
crops. The earlier rain god was Parjanya, who gave gentle rain to
allow the grass to grow, and sheltered the nomads with his clouds
from the scorching sun. Indra, on the other hand, grew strong by
forcibly partaking of the Soma juice; he then killed Vritra, the
Visvarupa, god of the clouds, who was also called *gotra*, protector
of the cows, and thus let free the waters that Vritra was with-
holding.

Now, Vritra was the son of Tvastar, the fire god who forged
thunderbolts for Indra. Tvastar is often associated with, and sometimes even identified with, Vishnu. The fluctuating relationship
between Tvastar-Vishnu and Indra is a perfect reflexion of the
vicissitudes of the Aryan community in the Indo-Gangetic plain.
Tvastar and Vishnu are often shown as assisting Indra in his
exploits, and at other times strongly opposing him. Tvastar and
Vishnu represent the Brahmin class, which sometimes sides with the
agricultural people represented by Indra, and at other times places
its weight on the side of the pastoral class. Vritra is said to be
the priest of the gods (*devas* and *asuras*, both in the same sense,
though later the latter term designates the demons). To him, honey,
wine and victuals were offered. Tvastar is embittered by the killing
of his son by Indra and so fights against him. At one time, Indra
is honoured as the highest of the gods, but slowly Vishnu takes
precedence over him.[18]

The scene is made more complex with the appearance of Krishna.
In the Vedas, there is mention of a Krishna Devakiputra, a sage.
In the *Mahabharata* also, Krishna appears as the counsellor of the
Pandavas against the Kauravas. This modest figure of Krishna in
the earlier portions of the *Mahabharata* shows that the Krishna in
myth arose, not in the northern Aryan centres where the bulk of
the epics was formed, but in the southern centres like Mathura
which at a later stage provided additional epic material, like the
Harivamsa Purana. Krishna was probably the non-Aryan chief
who marched against the Aryans with an army of ten thousand
men and was vanquished by Indra.

[17] *RV*, X, 72, 2.
[18] Cf. J. Gonda, *Aspects of Early Vishnuism* (Utrecht, 1954).

But in the elaborate Krishna story of the *Harivamsa Purana* and the *Bhagavata Purana*, he appears as the champion of the pastoral people against the agricultural class and the Brahmin priests who sided with them. In the *Harivamsa*, he dissuades his relatives from offering the annual sacrifices to Indra, because he was the god of the agricultural class; besides, the Brahmins profited most from these elaborate sacrifices. Instead, the pastoral class under the leadership of Krishna adorns the cows, takes them in procession through the hills and offers them sacrifice. Indra, angered by the denial of his annual festivities, comes down with thunderstorms and torrential rain to ruin the people and their cows. But Krishna, the avatar of Vishnu, snatches up a mountain and holds it for an umbrella over the whole farm. Indra is defeated and comes down begging for pardon and protection from Krishna, and thus peace is restored. From then on Krishna is the supreme deity, identical with Vishnu, from whom, in whom and by whom are all things. Krishna comes also as a compromise for the colour problem which plagued the Vedic period : the Vedas speak derogatively of the darker skin of the Dasyus, and Indra, the Aryan god, is luminous like lightning; Vishnu is whiter than the sea of milk over which he sleeps. Indra and Agni are said to be 'of a white complexion and to rise from below with bright rays to heaven'.[19] But in contrast, Krishna's beauty, which is capable of enrapturing the fifty thousand women of Dvaraka, is in his blue-black complexion, the colour of rain clouds.

This conflict of religious cultures and their eventual resolution is the underlying theme in a good number of Puranic stories. The story of Prahlada, described in several Puranas, is typical : the Daitya chief, Hiranyakasipu, defeats Indra and declares sovereignty over heaven and earth. However, his son Prahlada is an ardent devotee of Vishnu and speaks out against all political manoeuvres and social conflicts on which his father pitches all his success. All the frantic efforts of Hiranyakasipu to initiate his son in politics and make him change his allegiance to Vishnu are of no avail. Finally, Vishnu appears as a man-lion and kills Hiranyakasipu, and the cult of Vishnu is universally accepted. *Vishnu Purâna* extols this total surrender to the cult of Vishnu.[20]

[19] *RV*, VIII, 5, 10, 8.
[20] *VP*, Book I, *cc*. 17–20. Cf. Paul Haecker, *Prahlada, Werden und Wandlungen einer Idealgestalt* (Mainz, 1960).

The first instance of East-West encounter

A lesson to be drawn from these ups and downs of customs and cults, and the rise, fall and fusion of different gods, is the clear distinction between faith and tradition. In all the cultural and political conflicts, the quest for the absolute meaning of life and the cult of the Supreme remain unchanged. There is also a firmly rooted moral sense. Even the worshippers of phallic deities do not allow licence and debauchery. Though religion often serves as a pretext for the promotion of political ends, in the end, however, politics and social structures are taken over and transformed by religion.

The very fact that religious structures, including deities and cults, undergo radical changes shows that human expressions are inadequate to manifest the depth of faith. Expressions can vary from abstract philosophical conceptions to down-to-earth and crude experience of life and passions. Gods can be presented with all the moderation and refinement of culture or shown in the impressive manifestation of raw might. In his yearning for new forms of religious expression, man is striving for a comprehensive grasp of the divine phenomenon in human life. Religion deals with God and divine things. But, after all, it remains a human phenomenon. It is not for God, but for man, to enable him to attain the divine destiny through his own activity.

The cultural interaction between Aryans and pre-Aryans has a great importance as a first instance of the East-West encounter. The Aryans, who were of the same stock as the Greeks and the Nordic people of Europe, were western in outlook and thought-pattern in almost every respect. Their gods were different only in name from those of the Greeks. Their world vision was abstract and to a great extent rational, just like that of the Greeks. On the other hand, the pre-Aryans, with their crude fertility cults, phallic symbols and natural mysticism presented the typically oriental mentality. A real dialogue took place between them in the Indo-Gangetic plain, and the outcome saved and integrated the positive elements of both the religious cultures.

The Aryan culture came down from its speculative abstraction and detached rationalization to the level of the concrete. The nomadic Aryan became civilized and he realized the advantages of a settled and organized society. The pre-Aryans got out of their closed natural mysticism and awoke to the cosmic dimensions of religion. The drunken dance of the Indus Valley god of the animals evolved into the cosmic dance of Siva. The tribal fight of Krishna and other Dasyu leaders against the Aryan invaders slowly evolved into the Avataras of Vishnu, who appears in every age to re-establish the balance of good and evil, right and wrong. The gods of the Aryans left their heavenly places and became gods of men, and the animal gods of the pre-Aryans willingly accepted the subordinate role of being the official mythological vehicles of the heavenly gods. What is, perhaps, more important, a certain friend-ship between the races was achieved when everyone was integrated into a sacral community with definite places of identity and assigned distinctive roles in the comprehensive organization of the caste.

CHAPTER V

RELIGION AND SOCIETY

The emergence of a socially stratified and organized religious community on the Indian sub-continent is an instance of the mutual interaction between religion and society. Man seeks God from the natural context of his daily life. The available modes of satisfying his material needs set the pattern for the exercise of his religion. This emergence of the Hindu society in India involved the co-existence of various races and tribes, as well as of the nomadic pastoral community with the settled agricultural population.

The jungle man did not require to engage in the toils of tilling the land and planting the seed as long as he could support himself with the natural produce of the land. The Buddhist and Jainist prohibition against taking any life indicates the existence in ancient India of a primitive economy of bloodless food gathering. When a part of the people practised plough agriculture in the Indo-Gangetic plain, another section found enough food in the virgin forests through which the people wandered along with their cattle. Even today in several parts of India, tribes are found that seek their livelihood from fruits, nuts, berries, leafy vegetables, mushrooms and honey, gathered from the forests. Though these tribes have the same caste names as those of the neighbouring agricultural people, they still maintain their identity by abstaining from inter-marriage and other forms of contact with them. As shown by the pastoral people of the *Harivamsa Purana* and *Mahabharata*, this jungle culture had a feeling of superiority and a sense of greater freedom over the settled agricultural tribes. Both in the *Mahabharata* and the *Ramayana*, the heroes willingly accept long years of staying in the jungle in contrast to the greed and selfishness of the people who send them out from their rightfully owned property. Kalidasa's *Sakuntala* describes the peaceful and elevated life led

28

in the colony of sages in the jungle, away from the ambitions and quarrels of the city dwellers.

This jungle life of the tribes must have been the starting-point of caste system. As D. D. Kosambi says, 'the two major characteristics of the caste system—prohibitions against marriage outside the group and against acceptance of food from the hands of a stranger—are taboos that are typical of food-gathering societies'.[1] These food-gatherers established their closely-knit society with their own protective deities and their specially privileged priesthood.

Soon, the agricultural people established a sounder economic base, and, on account of their better food supply and greater security against diseases and other dangers, increased in number faster than the food-gatherers. They could easily afford to support a priestly class, which would also assume the task of mediation with their pastoral neighbours. For the wandering food-gatherers, however, their chiefs and leaders were also priests. When these two communities were eventually integrated, two classes of social leaders emerged—the Brahmin priests and the tribal chiefs. These became the two prominent classes in the caste system. Both were vested with a certain sacral character.

Race and caste

However, the influence of race distinctions in the evolution of the caste system cannot be neglected. *Varna,* colour, the traditional Sanskrit term for caste, occurs a great many times in the *Rig Veda.* Nevertheless, in the majority of contexts it does not designate any class organization; it merely indicates the superiority of the white Aryans over the dark-skinned Dasyus.[2] This race distinction should have given origin to distinction in occupations, and also in a final integration of groups and communities into a certain hierarchy of functions and places in the society. This diversity of functions, occupations and modes of life became the immediate and decisive factor in the formation of different classes and castes. According to *Aitareya Brahmana,* the Andhras, Pundras, Sabaras, Pulindas, and according to *Manu Smriti,* also the Dravidas, Kambojas, Yavanas, Sakas, Pahlavas, Cinas and Kiratas, were all originally Kshatriyas, but were later reduced to the lowest level of the caste scale because of their failure to perform the Vedic

[1] 'Living Pre-History in India', *The American Review,* XII, 41 (1967).
[2] *RV,* II, 12, 4; I, 179, 6; IX, 71, 2; III, 34, 9; IV, 16, 13.

samskaras.[3] Since most of these races are non-Aryan, it may be
more accurate to say that the Aryans first recognized them as
belonging to the warrior class, and later, when the Aryan power
was securely established, demoted them on the caste scale, as may
naturally be expected from a conquering race. Still, one thing is
clear : even these non-Aryan races were given a definite place in
the caste system.

The religious interpretation of caste

The religious interpretation of caste should have come much later
than its actual historical evolution. The earliest text in this respect
is the *Purushasûkta* of *Rig Veda* (X, 90), where the Brahmana
is said to originate from the mouth of the Purusha, the Rajanya
from his arms, Vaisya from his thighs and Sudra from his feet.
This sacred origin of the four classes is narrated in several books
of the Hindu scripture.[4] Though this narrative directly and expli-
citly shows the sacred origin of the classes, emphasis is also placed
on the functional distinction of the classes. The Brahmin, emerging
from the mouth, is to speak and teach; the Kshatriya represents
the arms of the cosmic person and therefore has to fight against
enemies and defend the country; the Vaisya, issuing from the thighs
of the Purusha, is entrusted with the work of cultivating the land;
the Sudra, coming from the feet of the ancient sacrificer, is commissioned for the menial works of the society.

This description of functions shows a class distinction based on
occupation. But the number of occupations far exceeds the number
of castes. If we except the priestly functions reserved to the
Brahmins and the lowest menial jobs done only by the lowest
classes, there is a great flexibility in jobs that can be taken up by
the castes. With the development of different jobs and the guild
mentality of people exercising the same trade, in the course of
time the number of castes and sub-castes multiplied into hundreds.
However, all these classes refer themselves to one or other of the
four major castes from a religious point of view. This means that
the functional aspect of caste is taken over by the sub-castes, while
the division into four castes remained as the symbol of the sacral
community of Hinduism. This sacral organization of society through

[3] *Aitareya Brahmana*, XXXIII, 6; *Manu Smriti*, X, 43–5.
[4] *RV*, VII, 104, 3; *AV*, VIII, 4, 13; V, 17, 9; II, 15, 4; *Satapatha
Brahmana*, V, 4, 6, 9; V, 5, 4, 9.

caste explains why the Brahmins received most of the attention in the question of caste, while the Vaisyas and Sudras were left with a bare mention in the Vedas.

The Brahmin

The Brahmana, coming forth from the mouth of the cosmic person, had the principal function of studying and reciting the sacred hymns. *Brahma*, in the *Rig Veda*, means prayer or hymn.[5] From this original meaning, it was easy to transfer it to the one who recited the hymns, though in the end a certain form of the word *Brahman* (n.) had to be reserved to denote the Supreme Reality, and another form *Brahma* (m.) to designate the personal creator, God. Brahmana or Brahmin became the name of the priest, the one possessing the ritual and magical power in relation to the deity, the custodian of the sacred scripture. According to *Taittirîya Brahmana*, Brahmin is god in visible form.[6] He is called the Vedic scholar (*vedavidvat, vedapâraga*), and the master of the three sastras, the three Vedas. *Manu Smriti* enjoins that 'a Brahmin should always and assiduously study the Veda alone; that is his highest *dharma;* everything else is inferior *dharma*'.[7] According to *Yajnavalkya Smriti* (I, 198), the preservation of the Vedas, safeguarding of *dharma*, and cult of the gods are the only reason for the creation of the Brahmins. The Brahmin who does not study or teach the Vedas or keep sacrificial fire becomes equal to the Sûdras.[8]

The communitarian aspect of the caste is shown by the injunction that the Brahmin had to live by gifts from other people. These gifts had to be free, not a remuneration, and had only to be given by worthy people. *Pratigraha*, or receiving gifts from the three higher classes, is worthier than the acquisition of wealth by officiating as a priest or by teaching.[9] On the other hand, accepting gifts from an unworthy person, or Sûdra, is, according to Manu, worse than the act of teaching him or officiating as a priest for him.[10] Hence, gifts to the Brahmin were not considered a remunera-

---

[5] *RV*, IV, 6, 11; VI, 52, 2; X, 105, 8; X, 141, 5; III, 53, 12.
[6] *RV*, I, 1, 2, 6, 7.
[7] *Manu Smriti*, IV, 147.
[8] *Vasishtha*, III, 1.
[9] P. V. Kane, *History of Dharmasastra*, Vol. II, Part 1 (Poona, 1941), p. 110, quoting from *Smriti Chandrika*, I, p. 179.
[10] *Manu Smriti*, X, 109–11.

tion for the services rendered by him, but an act of homage to the visible symbol of the sacred.

Brahmins as a sacred class had a certain hierarchy of order and functions. In the sacrificial ritual itself, there were the invokers (*hotri*), cantors (*udgâtri*) and the levites who performed the manual operations (*adhvaryu*). The priests engaged in the daily ministration of the temple formed another class, definitely of a lower order. Manu prescribed that a *devâlaka*, a Brahmin employed for service before the image in the temple for three years, was unfit to be invited for a sacrifice or for rites in memory of the dead.[11] *Manu Smriti* defines the role of the Brahmin community thus : 'Brahma directed that the duties of the Brahmins should be reading and teaching the Veda; sacrificing and assisting others to sacrifice, giving alms if they be rich, and receiving alms if they be poor.'[12] Thus, the importance of the Brahmin in the social organism was not in the service he rendered or the function he fulfilled, but rather in his position as teacher and guide and as representative of the sacred.

He was the symbol of spiritual authority, and in that respect was held in high esteem, even over the political power of the temporal rulers. The king had to appoint a Brahmin to be chief over all his ministers as his best counsellor, another as his Purohita, or family priest, and a third to perform sacrifices.[13] The judiciary mainly consisted of Brahmins, and a court of four Brahmins was called the Court of Brahma.[14] The king had to provide maintenance for the Brahmins, and when a Brahmin was well learned in the Vedas, he was to be exempted from taxation.[15] Several other special privileges were accorded to the priestly class,[16] which, as the literate *élite*, did not miss the chance to write a good many legends concerning its superhuman powers into the sacred books : for example, an angry Brahmin could, by his sacrifices and imprecations, exterminate kings with their troops, elephants and chariots.[17]

But, in spite of these legendary powers of the Brahmins narrated in books, reality was rather more prosaic. In court politics, when

[11] *Ibid.*, III, 152.
[12] *Ibid.*, I, 94–101.
[13] *Ibid.*, VII, 58–9; 78.
[14] *Ibid.*, VIII, 1, 9, 11.
[15] *Ibid.*, VII, 133–5.
[16] *Ibid.*, VIII, 380.
[17] *Ibid.*, IX, 313-5.

the court Brahmins could not muster enough strength to influence a king or dispose of an undesirable character, they had to end up in the unenviable position of humouring the whims of a monarch, as we find in stories like the *Malavikagnimitra* of Kalidasa. Since the Brahmin could not generally engage in lucrative business, he was often reduced to poverty. In that situation, he had to gain his livelihood by lawful gleaning and gathering and by what was given to him in alms and by tillage. Only in extreme distress could he engage in money-lending or in the professions of a Kshatriya or Vaisya.[18] But he could never engage in menial work, or sell flesh-meat or spirituous liquors.[19] Manu permitted the Brahmins to eat meat, provided the animals were ritually offered to the gods or consecrated by *mantras*.[20]

Thus, the Brahmins constituted the central factor in a sacral community, symbol of a pure and consecrated life. The spiritual paternity of the Brahmin is clearly set forth in the following Vedic quotation in *Vasishtha*:

> Of two kinds, forsooth, is the virile energy of a man learned in the Vedas: that which resides above the navel, and the other which below the navel descends downwards. Through that which resides above the navel, his offspring is produced, when he initiates Brahmanas, when he teaches them, when he causes them to offer oblations, when he makes them holy. By that which resides below the navel, the children of his body are produced. Therefore, they never say to a *srotriya*, who teaches the Veda, 'Thou art destitute of offspring'.[21]

The Kshatriyas

The ruling and fighting class, the Rajanya or Kshatriya, was probably the evolution of the tribal chieftains, whether they belonged to the Aryan groups, or came from the non-Ayran communities. According to Manu, the Creator commanded the Kshatriya 'to protect the people, to bestow gifts, to offer sacrifices, to study (the Veda) and to abstain from attaching himself to sensual pleasures'.[22] This duty to sacrifice was an integral part of his obligation as a householder to tend the sacrificial fire for himself.[23] The injunction to study is in reference to his obligation to

[18] *Ibid.*, IV, 1, 6; XI, 194–7.
[19] *Ibid.*, X, 81–9.
[20] *Ibid.*, V, 26–42.
[21] *Vasishtha*, II, 5, Sacred Books of the East, Vol. XIV, Part 2, p. 9.
[22] *Manu Smriti*, I, 89. [23] *Vasishtha*, II, 16.

rule the people in accordance with the scriptures. A Kshatriya is not supposed to teach, sacrifice for others, or accept gifts.[24] Still, we find in the Upanishads several kings like Ajatasatru, Janaka of the Videhas, Pravahana Jaivali, Asvapati Kaikeya and others, who are learned enough to instruct even Brahmins. The Kshatriya is asked to bear arms for protecting himself and others.[25]

Relationship between Brahmin and Kshatriya

Hindu scriptures have worked out a theory of co-existence and co-operation between Brahmin and Kshatriya in the government of the sacral community. There is no question of two swords, nor of one being the subordinate of the other. It is rather the co-responsibility of man and woman in the conjugal society. Priesthood is the husband, and royalty the wife. Here, it must be borne in mind that in the Hindu tradition, the maternal principle, the pregnant *Prakriti*, is the more effective and creative factor. The paternal principle initiates the process, but stands apart as the uninvolved witness, but actively vigilant about the whole evolution of the progeny.

The *Satapatha Brahmana* and *Aitareya Brahmana* draw upon this symbolism to explain the interrelationship between the priest and the king, and find a basis for it in the Vedic couples of Mitra and Varuna, Agni and Indra and Brihaspati and Indra. Here Mitra, Agni and Brihaspati represent the divine and priestly power, the male principle, while Varuna and Indra stand for the maternal and creative principle. Kingship is a trust committed to the royal power. 'Into thy hands, O Indra, I (Agni) commit the bolt,' reads the Vedic text.[26] The priestly authority representing eternal *Dharma*, the divine wisdom, stands independent; it does not depend on the royal power. But the royal power, to be effective, always has to be dependent on *Dharma*. This *Dharma*, or wisdom, is symbolized by Agni (fire) and Savitar (god of light). Wisdom merely indicates the path of action; it has no power to execute it. It is the function of the royal power to carry out and effect what is indicated by wisdom. Thus, Brihaspati is acclaimed in the Vedas as the 'far-seeing herdsman and pathfinder',[27] and Agni as the

[24] *Manu Smriti*, X, 77.
[25] *Ibid.*, VII, 87–99.
[26] *RV*, X, 52, 5; II, 11, 4.
[27] *RV*, II, 23, 6.

'Authentic Lord of the sky and earth; as it were, their herdsman'.[28] It is in the light of Agni that Indra, the royal power, should act. In the *Rig Veda*, Agni says: 'I in person go before thee . . . and if thou givest me my share, then shalt thou through me, O Indra, perform heroic deeds.'[29]

Satapatha Brahmana expresses the same idea, taking Mitra and Varuna for representatives of priestly and kingly powers: 'Mitra is the priesthood, and Varuna the nobility; and the priesthood is the conceiver, and the noble is the doer.'[30] They are like intellect and will. Intellect can function without the will, though it may not be very effective. But the will cannot function at all without the intellect. So the two got wedded for the success of both. Though sometimes a Brahmin may be without a king, 'it is quite improper that a king should be without a Brahmin'.[31] The principle behind this conjugal union is that real authority should not get involved in power politics, and that power should never rule absolutely. When power breaks loose from *Dharma*, the whole social order is destroyed.

SVADHARMA: CONCEPT OF PERSONAL MORALITY

Apart from the sacral authority of the Brahmins, the whole caste system may resemble a mere social organization, like the one presented in the Republic of Plato or the State of Hegel, in which particular persons are absorbed in a system and ordered for its common goal. In the matter of interdependence of classes, it functions like a feudal society. The persons in the lower rungs of society willingly remain in their position, because they have their identity and security. This was especially so in Indian society, since in the ancient system of village rule by *Pancâyats*, elected bodies of five, every class and section of the village community was represented. The higher castes had certain definite obligations towards the lower castes, and the lower castes had certain symbolic privileges and rights, on special occasions like marriage and festivities, by

---

[28] *RV*, I, 144, 6.
[29] *RV*, VIII, 100, 1.
[30] *Satapatha Brahmana*, IV, 1, 4.
[31] Cf. Ananda K. Coomaraswamy, *Spiritual Authority and Temporal Power in the Indian Theory of Government* (New Haven, Conn: American Oriental Society, 1942; reprint, New York: Kraus Reprint Corp., 1967), p. 87.

which they showed their right of belonging to the same community with the higher castes. In all these, caste society functioned like any other sociocentric or ethnocentric group.

What distinguished caste as a sacral community, and maintained the balance between community and the individual, was the concept of *svadharma*, or personal duty. Each individual has a unique rôle to fulfil in society. It is not dictated from the outside by an external authority, a written law or an abstract ideal, but rose from the very internal life of the sacral community. This vital rôle in the community constituted the immediate and total source of morality for a person. Exalted as the rôles of the Brahmin and the Kshatriya were, equally necessary were the Vaisya and the Sudra. *Svadharma* is one's total commitment to duty and to the sacral community. Nothing should draw one away from this commitment. The central point in the *Bhagavad Gîta* is this *svadharma*. The fault of Arjuna is that he is swayed by his sentiments for his kith and kin and considerations of pity and of worldly gain, and fails to realize his duty as a Kshatriya to fight. Sri Krishna represents the Superior Wisdom who guides Arjuna on the path of action.

Svadharma implies an action-oriented society. Everyone has to act. Inaction will be the end of life itself. Even the Creator has to act. But his action is not for any fruit or result. So, ideal activity should be disinterested and unselfish. Each one draws life from the community, and each one realizes from that very cosmic *rita* or harmony, one's particular condition in the whole as well as one's specific mission in life.

Hence, a great many western scholars have admitted and praised the high ideals of the Hindu caste system. Sidney Low speaks of the caste system as 'the main cause of the fundamental stability and contentment' by which India survived 'the shocks of politics and the cataclysms of nature'.[32] Similarly, Abbé Dubois, who spent several decades in India as a dedicated Christian missionary, wrote about caste as the happiest expression of Hindu legislation, which saved India from falling into a state of barbarism similar to that in which almost the whole of Europe was plunged in certain periods of history.[33]

[32] *Vision of India*, pp. 262–3, quoted by P. V. Kane, *op. cit.*, Vol. II, Part I, p. 20.
[33] *Ibid.*

Decadence of caste system

On the other hand, the caste system in India has also elicited the severest criticism from several writers. Some have characterized it as 'the most disastrous and blighting of all human institutions', and as 'the most baneful, hard-hearted and cruel social system that could possibly be invented for damning the human race'.[34] The reason for this criticism was that, in spite of the high ideals of the caste society as a sacral community, those principles never worked out in practice as happily as they sound. The distinction of the different classes and their duties, rights and privileges led to an elaborate legalism. Most of the Hindu law books devote large sections to the minute details of caste distinctions. Instead of being an incentive to human co-operation, it built up all kinds of fences and artificial barriers between man and man. Once the motive behind the particular legislation was lost sight of and their right spirit forgotten, these minute details of law became a repressive institution, applied with no consideration for the human beings involved.

There was certainly some flexibility in the caste rules, especially in the earlier periods, and one could move from one caste to another. As the story of Satyakâma Jâbâla and others show, a Brahmin was recognized as such much more by his qualities of soul than for his origin from Brahmin ancestors : Satyakâma is admitted by the Brahmin teacher as a Brahmin pupil for frankly admitting that he was born of an unknown father, while his mother was a servant girl in several families. Still, caste generally operated as an iron law that fixed a person's condition in life solely by his birth in a particular class. Not talent and personal effort, but the physical fact of generation was the factor which decided one's social position for ever.

The marriage between priesthood and royalty was never a happy one. Power is a great temptation for one who already enjoys authority and prestige, and the Brahmins often had recourse to power politics in order to impose their will on others. On the other hand, power tends to corrupt, and the rulers often succumbed to the urge to liberate themselves from the moral and religious authority of the Brahmins. In that situation, Brahmins were easily reduced to the position of court officials who had to be yes-men of the monarch to survive in court politics. Hence, their authority

[34] Maine and Sherring, quoted *Ibid.*, p. 21.

and influence on the king was very often rather nominal, and seldom effective.

The greatest blow to the caste system came with the fall of the Hindu kings. In Europe, with the fall of the Roman Empire and the Holy Roman Empire, ecclesiastical authority gained a certain political supremacy, and in the Muslim world, the Caliphs claimed to be both religious and temporal sovereigns. But in India, with no kings left to enforce their instructions and precepts, the Brahmins also lost their hold on the people in general. They isolated themselves from the common people as an *élite* body concerned only with spiritual matters—namely, study and interpretation of the Veda, worship conducted in the temples, and public festivals.

With this radical social change, caste society lost its aspect of a sacral community and the castes more or less became guilds, each concerned with defining and protecting its own individual rights. The Mughals did not pay much attention to these distinctions of colour and status within the closed Hindu community. Hence, even through the Muslim rule, castes were rather volatile and their boundaries flexible. We find several Brahmins as soldiers and officers in Akbar's army.

With the establishment of the British Raj, the caste system assumed the force of a legal code, interpreted and applied with a strictness that only the British administrators were capable of. So Sir Henri Sumner Maine, in his *Village Communities* (1890 ed., p. 57) could rightly make this statement : 'The true view of India is that, as a whole, it is divided into a vast number of independent, self-acting, organized social groups, trading, manufacturing, cultivating.'[35] Every one claimed the maximum of rights, privileges and immunities in the name of caste and appealed to all kinds of traditions. In this situation of interminable disputes and law suits, the British jurists tried to draw up an exhaustive list of castes and sub-castes with their well-defined rights and privileges. This ended up in thousands of castes, each one of which had the characteristics of an individual, namely, independence from others, self-acting autonomy, internal organization and a particular job or profession.

With the aspect of the sacral community lost sight of, the interdependence of classes was dissolved, the role and function in the

[35] Quoted by Louis Dumont, 'The Functional Equivalents of the Individual in Caste Society', *Contributions to Indian Sociology*, VIII (Paris : Mouton & Co., October 1965), p. 87.

attainment of a common sacred goal forgotten. The superiority of certain classes became a meaningless burden on the inferior classes who were looked upon with contempt by the more privileged classes. This naturally produced bitterness and resentment among various sections of the people. These social inequalities became incompatible with the democratic ideas of this century. So India, with its secular constitution and democratic institutions, is fast moving towards a classless society.

Conclusion

However, caste had a unique role in the history of India. It was the one important factor that maintained the cultural unity of India through the vicissitudes of politics. It provided India with the spiritual outlook that has been its characteristic feature in facing every social, economic and political problem.

The greatest contribution of caste is the sense of hierarchy it engendered in the minds of the people. Counterbalancing the individualism implied in *svadharma*, caste emphasizes the principle of interdependence of the higher and the lower. Equality and hierarchy are primary realities of social order, and have to be properly balanced in a harmonious society. Egalitarianism emphasizes the freedom and responsibility of each individual and his transcendence over society itself. Hierarchy, on the other hand, stands for an orientation to the proper goal which is common for all men.

In India, the theory of *karma-samsâra*, of merit and transmigration, considerably reduced the importance of the particular. Transmigration stands for the totality of the human phenomenon, embracing and extending through all manifestations of life, from the lowest particle of plant life to the highest Brahman, the absolute reality. It is the same dynamic reality that manifests itself in every particular. At the same time, *svadharma* states that each individual is in his proper place on account of his free and rational recognition of the moral ideal. How far the theory of *karma-samsâra* influenced caste system is not easy to determine. Whatever its influence, caste worked as a balance between the fatalism of transmigration and the meaningless freedom of the individual. Though it never worked as a perfect social system, it presented an ideal for Indian tradition to reconcile individual freedom and responsibility with a sense of hierarchy, and a feeling of common purpose and goal for all men.

CHAPTER VI

JAINISM AND BUDDHISM—THEIR CONTRIBUTION TO INDIAN RELIGIOUS CULTURE

Revolt against Brahmanical authority and ritualistic religion could naturally be expected, not only from the lower rungs of the caste ladder, but also from the Kshatriya group which was the principal rival of the Brahmins. More especially, the pre-Aryan people of India, driven by the newcomers to the East and to the South, were waiting for an opportunity to reassert their traditional religious values. These groups, which did not accept the authority of the Vedas were called *nâstikas*, non-believers, by the Brahmins and in general were designated by the title Srâmanas.

There were many such groups in the beginning, before they were all absorbed into the two main religious groups of Jains under Mahavira, and Buddhists under Siddhartha Gautama. Such groups had, however, certain common traits which brought out their opposition to the Vedic religion.

(1) They all challenged the authority of the Vedas and refused to worship the Vedic gods. This would have been the reason why they were styled as non-believers and atheists.

(2) They admitted into their religious communion all persons, irrespective of class and caste. This was an evident reaction to the hegemony of the Brahmins in the caste system. Thus, it emerged as a revolution of the common people against the privileged nobles.

(3) In the place of the ritualistic and legalistic rules of the caste society, in which *svadharma*, one's particular role and duty in a situation, and *varnasramadharma*, the duty imposed by one's state and caste, predominated, these groups developed ethical systems. These systems of morality formulated basic principles of right and wrong, good and evil, equally binding on all men.

(4) They all demanded a more detached life than that proposed

40

by the Brahmanical religion. The Vedic community had a rational outlook on life, with a social organization planned for efficiency. In its view, *artha* (wealth), and *kâma* (the pleasures of life), were goals of life, equally important as the practice of virtues and liberation itself. The Srâmana religious sects had a more pessimistic view of earthly life and emphasized the importance of detachment. This came naturally from a comparison of the relative values of soul and body, spirit and matter, worldly life and the life beyond death.

(5) Another important aspect of the religious life of the Srâmanas was the view of asceticism as a way of life undertaken at any time after the *brahmacharya*, or minor age. In the Brahmanic Hinduism, *vânaprastha*, or ascetic life in the forest, was only a phase of man's life coming at the end of his career, as a preparation for death.

(6) That the religious literature of these groups was written mostly in regional languages, or Prakrits, and not in Sanskrit, shows their opposition to the Brahmanical language. Jainism and Buddhism were faithful to this tradition. Mahavira preached in the dialect called Artha-Mâgadhi, and Buddhist scriptures were originally in Pâli.

HISTORICAL EVOLUTION OF THE MOVEMENT

Reaction to Brahmanical teaching is shown in the tenets of the early religious teachers known in Buddhist records as the six heretics, namely Pûrana Kâssappa, Pakudha Kaccâyana, Makkhali Gosala, Ajita Kesambalin, Sanjaya Belatthiputta, and Nigantha Nataputta.[1] The first, judging by his Sanskrit name, Pûrna Kâsyapa, seems to have been a Brahmin wise man. He taught a theory of non-action. According to him, 'in giving alms, in offering sacrifices, in self-mastery, in control of the senses, and in speaking truth, there is neither merit nor increase of merit'.[2] His was evidently a position contradicting Brahmanical ritualism and the systematized ascetical practices prescribed by certain Brahmanical schools.

Opposition to Brahmanical ritualism and the mystical meaning it ascribed to things seems to have led people like Pakudha

[1] Cf. Rhys Davids, *Dialogues of the Buddha,* Sacred Books of the Buddhists, Vol. I (1923), p. 220, for a list of ten herectical sects.
[2] Rhys Davids, *op. cit.,* pp. 69–70.

Kaccâyana to a theory of eternal elements. Kaccâyana postulated seven elements: earth, water, fire, air, pleasure, pain and the soul. Hence, it is incorrect to speak of things, which are merely aggregates of these elements. There is no slayer and no slain, no hearer and no speaker. Pleasure and pain produce the combination of elements.[3]

The *Ajivaka* school of wandering mendicants, claiming Makkhali Gosala as leader, practised an extreme form of asceticism. Their mode of life itself was an open challenge to the well-ordered and dignified religious life taught by the Brahmins. All these isolated groups were finally overshadowed by the two great religious movements of Jainism and Buddhism, which exerted their influence all over India, and even to countries far beyond its confines.

JAINISM

Mahavira, known as Vardhamana, was the founder of Jainism. When he died in 527 B.C., he left behind him a well-organized religious group. It was more like a religious order than a popular religion. Towards the common people, Jainism was rather liberal. They had only to follow the five vows of non-violence, truthfulness, and abstention from theft, adultery and greed. For the householders, these were all *anuvratas,* or minor vows. For example, a householder had to fully abstain from intentionally causing injury to others and had to take as much care as was practically possible from accidentally causing harm and from occasioning injury, either by the practice of his occupation or in self-defence. But the monk had to observe these and the *mahavratas,* or major vows, as well. He had to abandon completely all worldly possessions, cease to dwell under a roof, and practise the twenty endurances like hunger, thirst, cold, heat, mosquito-bite, beating, begging, and the rest. He was to practise *ahimsa,* or non-violence, scrupulously, walk only during day, lest he should trample some living creature under foot in the dark, avoid in his speech all censure of others, self-praise, and talk about women, kings, thieves and eatables.

Jaina philosophy emphasized the incomprehensibility of reality. The logic of sevenfold affirmation shows that we cannot comprehend anything by our statement about it because, concerning any given thing, it is possible to make seven statements which are

[3] B. M. Barua, *A History of Pre-Buddhistic Indian Philosophy* (Calcutta University, 1921), pp. 283–4.

contradictory, and yet all true in certain respects and, at the same time, all false as well in other respects : something is; it is not; it is and is not; it is indescribable; it is and is indescribable; it is not and is indescribable; it is, is not and is indescribable. None of these statements comprehends the thing as it is. This is called the *syâdvâda*, or the 'may-be' theory. Therefore, the only reasonable course of action is to take different partial approaches to a thing from different angles or aspects. By the co-ordination of these aspects, a clearer view of the thing may be attained. This co-ordination of approaches is called *saptanaya*, the convergence of seven approaches on the same object. They are : generality, particularity, time, usage of language and grammar, conventional meaning, original sense, and the final co-ordinated view.

According to the Jaina view, reality is uncreated and eternal, and, at the same time, characterized by origination, decay, and permanence : it appears and disappears in the midst of permanence.

Against the background of such a labyrinthine philosophy, the only reasonable course of procedure was to place the accent on the individual's own spiritual perfection. On this spiritual path, Jainism distinguished fourteen stages, *gunasthânâs*, starting from the first, where the aspirant is steeped in falsehood and moves forward through a slow process of purification. At the fourth stage, *samyag darsana*, or right outlook, is attained. The fifth stage brings right faith. By the seventh stage, slackness in conduct is eliminated. Extraordinary spiritual powers, which are attained by a control of the passions, manifest themselves at the eighth stage. The eleventh stage marks the removal of all delusion, and perfect knowledge is the feature of the thirteenth. However, an aspirant is freed from all mortal coils and *samsâra* itself and becomes a *siddha* only at the fourteenth stage.[4]

Thus, Jainism tried to emphasize the centrality of the individual in religion, and the importance of personal sanctification. All ritual and social organizations should contribute towards this goal of the individual. In this way, these religious movements counterbalanced the caste organization which reduced the human person to a mere unit in the society. Jainism preached equality, *sâmâiya*, as its basic religious attitude.

On the other hand, Jainism also provided for the sense of hier-

[4] Hiralal Jain, 'Jainism: Its History, Principles and Precepts', *The Cultural Heritage of India*, Vol. I (Calcutta, 2nd ed., 1958), pp. 400–13.

archy through the concept of the *parameshtins*, persons who had attained freedom and knowledge to a supereminent degree and thereby became authoritative teachers. There are *parameshtins* of several different grades and degrees. One could obtain this title even before attaining complete liberation, namely, as *sâdhu*, the mendicant preacher, *upâdhyâya*, instructor, and *âcarya*, teacher, differentiated according to the level of detachment and knowledge acquired by the individual teacher. But the highest teacher is a *Tirthankara*, who is like a divine incarnation for his age, proclaiming universal peace and harmony. All these teachers deserve reverence and worship from the devotees.

Later, Jainism split up into several sects; the two major groups are the *Digambaras*, who emphasize nudity as the symbol of total detachment, and the *Svetambaras*, who are known for their white dress. At one time Jainism spread all over India. It has exerted considerable influence in the religious tradition of India.

BUDDHISM

Buddhism was the strongest religious movement dominating the whole Orient. It did so over a full millennium. From the sixth century B.C. to well beyond A.D. 700, it dominated the whole subcontinent of India, and from there extended its influence to Tibet, China and Japan in a northerly direction, and to Ceylon, Burma and the whole of South-East Asia, including the islands of Indonesia. In these countries even today, Buddhism is the source of inspiration for their age-old religious culture. It not only provided the people with faith and inspiration, but also shaped a consistent and comprehensive mode of life that gave rise to unique styles in painting and architecture.

The popular appeal of Buddhism was in its concentration of attention on the spiritual preoccupations of the common man. Ordinary people could not appreciate the esoteric ritualism of the Brahmins. Besides, Brahmanic religion was rather expensive, and made excessive demands on the credulity of the people. Buddhist literature contains prolonged invectives against the money-making and prestige-gaining malpractices of the Brahmins.[5] In contrast, Buddhist teaching was simple and ethical : abstain from evil, accumulate what is good, and purify the mind.[6] Gautama Sid-

[5] Cf. *Tevijja Sutta,* Sacred Books of the East, Vol. XI, pp. 192–200.
[6] *Dhammapada,* 183.

dhartha started from the legitimate aspirations of man, and showed that all of them could be fulfilled only by righteous conduct and by the quest of the ultimate meaning of life. If one should desire to become popular, to receive the necessaries of life, to do good to others, to conquer discontent and lust, to be victorious over danger and dismay, and 'to realize the hopes of those spiritual men who live in the bliss which comes, even in this present world', then 'let him fulfil all righteousness, let him be devoted to that quietude of the heart which springs from within, let him not drive back the ecstasy of contemplation, let him look through things, let him be much alone'.[7] This shift of emphasis from conformity to caste rules and from social propriety to personal righteousness and quietude of the heart was, in practice, the liberation of the common people, the low castes and the outcastes from the hegemony of the Brahmins.

Gautama Buddha belonged to the race of the Vrisalas, probably a non-Aryan group. He is referred to by the Brahmins as Srâmana Gautama.[8] He was the son of a king. This was indicative of a social and religious revolution headed by the ruling class, which sought the support of the common people against the nobles, the Brahmins. In Buddhism, anyone, irrespective of caste or colour, could be admitted to the *samgha*, the order of the monks, but the Brahman was still the ideal sage. However, one became a Brahman, not by mere birth, but by the personal achievement of sanctity. The *Bhikkus*, or monks of the Buddhist order, are often styled Brahmanas.[9]

This emphasis on individual freedom and responsibility also led to the emancipation of women under the auspices of Buddhism. They were raised to an equal status with men. Gautama allowed his aunt and nurse, Gotamid Prajapati, to become initiated as a nun, and he gave the nuns rules of religious conduct.[10] In Buddhist literature, women often appear as lay helpers ministering to the material needs of the monks and nuns,[11] and as wealthy hosts entertaining illustrious Buddhist teachers like Nagasena.[12]

[7] *Akangkheyya Sutta*, 3–19, Sacred Books of the East, Vol XI (Oxford, 1881; Delhi, 1965), pp. 210–8.
[8] *Tevijja Sutta*, 7, Sacred Books of the East, Vol. XI, p. 169.
[9] *The Mahavajja*, Sacred Books of the East, Vol. XIII, pp. 77–9.
[10] *Vinaya Pitaka*, II, 253ff.
[11] *Ibid.*, I, 290–4.
[12] *Milinda Panha.*

This spirit of freedom, motivated by the Buddhist ideal of universal amity, extended even to the animal kingdom. In the Buddhist paintings found in the Ajanta caves and elsewhere, we find all kinds of animals gathered together in friendship and harmony around the Bodhisattva. This was, on the one hand, a sublimation of the animal cults prevalent among the non-Aryan tribes, and, on the other, a protest against the killing of animals for sacrifice and for food sanctioned by the Brahmanical religion. Nevertheless, Buddha did not go to the extremism of the Jaina ascetics. He only forbade his monks 'knowingly to make use of meat killed purposely for them'. He said : 'I allow you, monks, fish and meat that are quite pure in these respects : if they have not been seen, heard or suspected to have been killed on purpose for a monk.'[13]

The popular aspect of Buddhism is borne out by the three objects in which a devotee had to take refuge—namely, *Buddha, Dhamma* and *Samgha*; he had to submit himself to the teacher, observe the rules of righteousness, and adhere to the community of monks. Against the danger of individualism in an atmosphere of freedom, veneration of the *Tathâgata*, the teacher, who had attained illumination, constituted a safeguard to preserve the sense of hierarchy. The *Tathâgata* is the sure guide on the spiritual path. '*Tathâgata* is born into the world, a fully Enlightened One, blessed and worthy, abounding in wisdom and goodness, happy with knowledge of the world, unsurpassed as a guide to erring mortals, a teacher of gods and men, a Blessed Buddha'.[14]

Similarly, the pattern of right conduct is a practical approach for regulating the life of the ordinary man. Gautama was against all abstract discussion concerning existence, nature and other metaphysical topics. When a man is wounded by an arrow, he does not stop to discuss the metal out of which the arrow was made, the caste of the man who shot it, and so on, but he is only anxious to have the arrow taken out as soon as possible and to apply the necessary medicines to the wound. So also, instead of discussing the existence and nature of God and of the soul, a person desirous of liberation should concentrate his attention on the right attitudes. These attitudes are faith, vigour, mindfulness, concentration and wisdom. One having faith draws near; he gives ear and hears *Dhamma*

[13] *Vinaya Pitaka,* I, 238.
[14] *Tevijja Sutta,* 46, Sacred Books of the East, Vol. XI, p. 187.

and tests the meaning of what he hears, and it pleases him. With mindfulness and zeal, he weighs the courses of action and strives resolutely to realize the highest truth, and through wisdom he understands its details.[15]

The institution of the *Samgha*, the order of the monks and nuns, constitutes an *élite* group that serves as a bulwark for the whole religious movement, providing unity and direction. Hence, unity is one of the basic requisites of the *Samgha*. 'Do not let there be a schism in the Order,' exhorts Buddha. 'He who splits an Order that is united sets up demerit that endures for an aeon and he is boiled in hell for an aeon. But he who unites an Order that is split sets up sublime merit and rejoices in heaven for an aeon.'[16]

The philosophy of Buddhism

Buddhism had a very simple philosophy, summarized in three words : *anâtman, anitya* and *duhkha* : there is no permanent individual soul; everything is fleeting and non-eternal; life itself is beset with suffering. This existence itself is a composite of parts, all arising out of craving. Owing to ignorance, and conditioned by it, there originate the *Samskârâ*, the dynamic residue of actions. Consciousness is formed and conditioned by that residue. From consciousness emerge mind and body; conditioned by them are the sense fields, which condition the impressions and feelings. Feeling conditions the craving. Craving is the root of action, and of rebirth. From birth originate grief, sickness, old age and death.[17] Hence, only by stopping ignorance can the whole process be stopped. This process of ignorance leading to bodily existence and existence leading to ignorance is known as *bhâvacakra*, the cycle of existence. Later commentators on Buddha's sayings have elaborated the factors coming in this cycle. According to Buddhaghosha, ignorance and the residue of past actions produce knowledge, name and form (*nâmarûpa*), the six sense-doors (*shathâyatana*), sense contact (*sparsa*), experience of pleasure and pain (*vedanâ*), grasping (*upâdâna*), craving (*trishna*), and the becoming of the new existence. The various factors, including the body of the four elements and senses,

[15] *Majjima Nikaya*, I, 479–80.
[16] *Vinaya Pitaka*, II, 184–98.
[17] *Ibid.*, I, 1, 1; *Mahavajja*, I, 1, 2, Sacred Books of the East, Vol. XIII, pp. 76–7.

feeling, conceptual knowledge, synthetic mental states and consciousness in their interdependence (*paticca samuppanna*), constitute what is called *skandha*, or trunk of the tree of life. In this structure *vinnâna*, or consciousness, is like a watchman at the middle of the cross-roads, beholding all that come from any direction.[18]

To plan an escape from this conditioned existence, attention should be directed to three levels in particular : the psychic, rational and behavioural spheres. Liberation on the level of behaviour involves the practice of virtues, or *sîla*; rational knowledge brings *pannâvimutti*; liberation of consciousness is *cetovimutti*. This three-fold liberation is attained through faith, knowledge and concentration. Simple faith leads to moral action and piety, and produces religious conviction. This rational faith leads to liberation of knowledge itself, and fullness of consciousness.

Karmasamsâra, or merit and rebirth, is a doctrine which Buddhism holds in common with Hinduism. *Karma*, or actions of a previous life, determine the condition of the new birth. This is resorted to as the sole explanation for the inequalities among men.

The final escape from this conditioned existence is called *nirvâna*. With *nirvâna*, one attains the complete cessation of *trishna*, or craving; it is totally renounced; this is freedom.

Philosophical Buddhism

Buddhism was more of a religious movement than a religion, in the strict sense generally given to this term. For several hundred years, even after the death of Gautama Buddha, Buddhism had no official religious texts to depend upon. Hence, the course of the movement depended upon the united will of the *samkha*, the assembly of the monks. But dissensions soon arose, and within a few hundred years of its existence, Buddhism split up into several branches with a good many sub-sects, none of which made any significant contribution to the religion itself. The first division came around 400 B.C., arising out of certain new opinions advocated by a few monks from the East. A council of the monks at Vesali decided against them, but they held a rival meeting and called themselves the *Mahâsâmkhikas*, or people of the great council. The conservative group was known as *Teravâda*, or the *Sthaviravada* school. In the course of the next two hundred years, both these schools split up into further sub-sections. A reconciliatory attempt

[18] *Milinda Panha*, 62, 8.

made by King Asoka in the third century B.C. did not have a lasting effect.

Soon, the divisions had to be justified by doctrinal differences, and so philosophical explanation of Buddha's teachings started. The conservative group, or the *Teravâda*, was, from the second century onwards, known as *Hetuvâdins* or *Sarvâstivâdins*. They defended the real existence of all things. The liberal school was known in the later tradition as *Mahayana*, the group of the great vehicle, in contrast to the *Hinayana*, the lesser vehicle, a name ascribed to the opposite group. The *Mahayana* produced two philosophical schools, the *Yogâcâra*, which proposed a sort of idealism known as *vijnânavâda*, and the *Madhyamikas*. When the *Yogâcâras* admitted the reality of knowledge, the *Madhyamikas* proposed *Sûnyavâda*, or void theory, which stated that no positive affirmation can attain the real nature of consciousness. Nagarjuna was the chief proponent of the *Sûnyavâda* philosophy, but the trend of thought itself dates back to the earlier period of Buddhism. The theory of *pratityasamutpâda*, or dependent origination, implies that a thing *is* only by the interdependence of its constituent factors. When their co-existence is dissolved, the factors have no independent existence of their own. But knowledge of a thing is what is gained by an analysis of it into its component parts. Since, by the dissolution of the components, the parts also cease to exist, what remains is the *sûnyatâ*, or void. As Nagasena explains to King Milinda, a chariot is neither the wheels, nor the axle nor other parts, but the dependent co-existence of the parts thereby constituting the whole. When separated from the whole, they are no longer parts.

Nagarjuna raises this discussion from the popular level to the sphere of consciousness itself. The reality of consciousness is not in structures, conceptual patterns or causal relationships. All these only put together and interrelate the things of our experience. Everything that falls within our experience is structured, conditioned and limited. Hence, it cannot be pure conditionless reality. By affirmations, we merely prolong the series of structures, but projecting them to any extent does not get us beyond the field of structures. Hence, trying to reach reality by our affirmations is like attempting to raise oneself by one's shoe strings.

This does not imply that Nagarjuna's philosophy is purely negative. His philosophy of consciousness is truly positive. However, according to him, the strongest affirmation of consciousness is deny-

ing everything that can be affirmed about it. When all structures
and conceptual forms are excluded, the resulting void, or *sûnyatâ*,
will be a reality beyond the field of experience.

THE CONTRIBUTION OF BUDDHISM TO THE INDIAN RELIGIOUS TRADITION

Buddhism almost disappeared from India by the Middle Ages,
yet it made certain lasting contributions to Indian religious tradition, and the importance of these cannot be overestimated.

First of all, Buddhism opened out a world vision in place of the
narrow social thought of the caste system. Buddhism was the first
world religion with a missionary zeal. Its missionaries set forth from
India in all directions. King Asoka, who ruled India in the third
century B.C., once he was converted to Buddhism, manifested a rare
religious enthusiasm. As his rock, cave and pillar edicts bear witness,
he repented over his wars of military conquest, which involved the
death of several hundred thousand people. In the place of such
digvijaya, or conquest of countries, which the Kshatriya princes held
as their ideal, Asoka set forth as his goal a *dharmavijaya*, conquest
by moral teaching. He claims that his religious message had reached
even the remote kingdoms of Rome and Egypt. Hinduism did not
encourage missionary work. Buddhism was a missionary religion
which welcomed everyone, without distinction of race and caste,
into its community of faith. The *Mahayana* (the great vehicle)
Buddhism was so called because its Buddhas who attained liberation,
instead of enjoying *nirvâna* for themselves, opted to remain in
bodily existence till all men could attain the same liberation.

The spirit behind this missionary zeal was universal love, the
core of Buddha's message. *Karuna*, or compassion for suffering
humanity, persuaded Gautama to leave his royalty in search of a
way of liberation, and after his illumination prodded him on his
long preaching journeys to communicate his realization to all men.
Ahimsa, or non-violence, was not a mere negative concept for him.
It involved *maitri*, loving kindness, for all men, and friendship with
the whole creation. As *Dhammapada* states, 'Hatred has never put
an end to hatred. Loving kindness puts an end to hatred. This is
the eternal law'.[19] The Buddhist *Jataka* stories contain a good many
tales that depict even animals sacrificing themselves selflessly for

[19] *Dhammapada.*

the sake of others. These legends often exaggerate heroism in order to accentuate the ideal of charity.[20]

Similarly, the Buddhist idea of the *Samkha,* the monastic order, introduced a new sense of the community. In Hinduism, the Brahmin was too lonely a sage to be an integral part of the common people. The Brahmin class formed an *élite* group, rather than a real community. The ascetics who betook themselves to the forests towards the end of their lives were anchorites who isolated themselves from the community. The *Rishis,* or sages, who were well known for their holiness, were remote models and often forbidding ideals; only rarely did they come out in public to instruct and inspire the common people. The Buddhist *Samkha,* on the other hand, was in the midst of the people, their monasteries were built by the people and were supported by the wealthy. The monks, in return, considered themselves obliged to help the community by their spiritual ministrations.

Buddhism, as a religious movement that started among the common people under the leadership of the ruling class, deeply influenced the life of the common man. It made a lasting impression on the religious tradition of India. The values brought to the forefront by Buddhism could neither be ignored nor wiped out by the later Hindu revival. They have remained an integral part of Indian tradition.

[20] Cf. Henri de Lubac, *Aspects of Buddhism,* trs. George Lamb (London: Sheed and Ward, 1953), pp. 15–52.

CHAPTER VII

PHILOSOPHICAL HINDUISM

The Religion of the Upanishads

That Vedic Hinduism could stage a come-back after an eclipse of over a millenium under the predominance of Buddhism is a matter of great wonder for many. Why did Buddhism decline, and how was Hinduism to revive? These are difficult questions to be solved, and a single solution may not be adequate. Evidently, there were several factors, among which historical vicissitudes and sociological reaction were important. Perhaps an important part in this dramatic transition from Buddhism to Hinduism should be ascribed to philosophy. Buddhism was a religious movement based on intuition. It had no solid rational philosophy to fall back upon. When it developed a philosophy, it was too removed from the religion of the common man to exert any appreciable influence. After the heyday of original thinking, led by Nagarjuna, Asanga and Asvaghosha, Buddhist philosophy deteriorated into abstract logic and sophistry.

On the other hand, in the case of Hinduism, the groundwork of a solid rational philosophy had already been laid in the Vedas, and the Upanishads had elaborated its main lines of thinking. Though this philosophical tradition was to a great extent lost sight of during the period of decadence, at a sober moment Hindu thinkers could always go back to the Upanishads. Even the Buddhist philosophers, in the elaboration of their systems, had drawn heavily from the Upanishads. At the weakest moment of Buddhism, namely towards the eighth century A.D., Hinduism produced some of its greatest geniuses, including Gaudapada and Sankaracharya. These not only assumed the positive elements of Buddhist philosophy, but also, by their interpretation of the Upanishads, showed that these fully belonged to the Hindu tradition. This consistent philosophical tradition is the great asset of Hinduism. I shall briefly indicate in this chapter the main lines of this philosophical

Hinduism, as presented in the Upanishads. From this discussion, we shall point out the main distinguishing characteristics of the Hindu philosophical tradition, leaving for subsequent chapters the discussion of the particular lines of speculation later developed in the various schools of thought.

THE PROBLEM OF KNOWLEDGE AND REALITY

Of the various points discussed in the Upanishads, the intimate relation between knowledge and reality is the most fundamental and comprehensive one. Religious thought in the Upanishads starts from the experience of human bondage, which primarily consists in ignorance. Hence, the principal concern is to attain knowledge in order to get rid of the enslaving ignorance. But this knowledge has to be constant and immutable, otherwise it can only lead to disillusionment and disappointment by its subsequent modifications. Such a stable knowledge cannot be attained by sense experience, which by its very nature is fickle. Nor can generalizations from sense experience provide any better stability. The only available avenue for arriving at immutable truth is *sabda*, the revealed doctrine of the Vedas. But even this *sabda* has to yield its wealth of knowledge through internal realization, in a way identifying the knower with the immutable reality.

This Supreme Reality is the one goal of all desire for knowledge; its realization brings with it the liberating illumination that excludes all change and modification. Hence, that Supreme Reality should be pure, immutable and infinite consciousness. 'He who knows Brahman as real (*satya*), knowledge (*jnâna*), infinite (*ananta*), residing in the cave of the heart and in the highest heaven, he obtains all desires.'[1] The mystic name of this Supreme Reality is '*idam-dra*', self-seeing.[2] He is the One in whom everything else is known.[3] Through him 'the unheard becomes heard, the unthought of becomes thought of, and the unknown becomes known'.[4] He is 'the seer of seeing . . . the hearer of hearing . . . the understander of understanding'.[5]

The principal concern of the Upanishads is to direct all minds

[1] *Tait Up*, II, 1.
[2] *Tait Up*, III, 1.
[3] *Chând Up*, VII, 17; *Brih Up*, IV, 5, 6.
[4] *Chând Up*, VI, 1, 4.
[5] *Brih Up*, III, 4, 2.

to this infinite consciousness.[6] Everything else, even the shining disc
of the Sun in the sky, and the god of light, Pushan, only hide the
supreme consciousnesss. The seeker after knowledge should go
beyond these in order to attain realization of the Supreme Truth.[7]
This realization cannot be achieved through much reading or discussion, nor through much hearing. The Supreme Consciousness
should manifest itself to the one who seeks after it.[8] When one can
see everything else in that supreme light, 'the knot of the heart is
loosened, and all one's doubts are solved'.[9]

THE SUPREME SELF AND THE INDIVIDUAL SOUL

This uncompromising transcendence of the Supreme Consciousness is brought down to the level of practical life by an equal
emphasis on its immanence in finite beings. The Self which is
infinite and immutable consciousness is greater than the greatest of
the physical universe, yet it is subtler than the subtle, and resides
in the heart of every creature. Only one who is desireless and has
controlled his passions can see the glory of the Self.[10] This Self is
bodiless among the bodies, and permanent in the midst of the
impermanent.[11] He is the ear of the ear, the mind of the mind,
speech of speech, life of life and eye of the eye—in other words,
the impeller of all man's knowledge.[12] Only through the light of
Self does one even sit down.[13] He is the one light of all that shines.[14]

The Supreme Self is the *antaryâmin*, the inner controller who
governs this world and the next and all things.[15] He is, as it were,
a string on which all beings are strung into a garland. 'This one is
the Lord of all (*sarvesvara*); this one is the omniscient; he is the
inner controller; he is the womb; he is truly the place of origin and
dissolution of all things.'[16] A singular way of showing his intimacy
to the beings, for the Upanishads, is to state that he resides in the

[6] *Mûnd Up*, I, 1, 5; *Svet Up*, VI, 19; *Ken Up*, II, 13.
[7] *Brih Up*, V. 15; *Isa Up*, 1.
[8] *Mûnd Up*, III, 2, 3; *Kath Up*, I, 2, 7–9, 23.
[9] *Mûnd Up*, II, 2, 8.
[10] *Kath Up*, I, 2, 20.
[11] *Kath Up*, I, 2, 22.
[12] *Ken Up*, I, 1–2.
[13] *Brih Up*, IV, 3, 6.
[14] *Kath Up*, 2, 15; *Svet Up*, VI, 14; *Mûnd Up*, II, 2–10.
[15] *Brih Up*, III, 7, 1.
[16] *Mândy Up*, 6.

space within the heart, though he is the Lord of all, and king of all.[17]

Already in the Vedas, the word *îsâna* indicates one gifted with power and energy.[18] Indra is *îsâna* because he rules the universe by his energy.[19] In earlier usage, the form *îsvara* was reserved to designate the king, the temporal ruler, but later, perhaps through the influence of the Siva-Mahesa cult, Isvara came to designate the Supreme Lord, the Lord of everything.[20] Isvara rules all things, principally by his intelligence. According to the *Svetasvatara Upanishad*, the Supreme Person, the instigator of existence, is the great Lord and light-imperishable,[21] yet his knowledge is all-comprehending. He embraces the whole visible universe with 'a hand, a foot on every side, on every side an eye and head and face'.[22] In the creation of the universe, after having created the Yatis,[23] the Isa, the great Atman (*mahâtman*), exercises universal lordship.[24] 'He is the world-protector', declares the *Kaushitaki Upanishad*. 'He is the World Sovereign (*lokâdhipati*). He is the Lord of all.'[25]

In relation with this Supreme Atman, the human person finds himself in a dual relationship. On the one hand, man has to realize that all that is good in him, all that is pure and without imperfection (like selfhood and consciousness) has its ground and source in the Supreme Lord. Hence, the Lord is the Ultimate Atman. On the other hand, he has to admit the infinite distance between his limited, individual selfhood and the Supreme Self. According to the *Brihadâranyaka Upanishad*, the individual self is the trace of the All 'for, by it, one knows this All. Just as, verily, one might deduce a person by a footprint'.[26] In the words of the *Svetasvatara Upanishad*, 'with the nature of the self, as with a lamp, a practiser of yoga beholds here the nature of Brahman'.[27] The aim of all Upanishadic teaching is to lead human beings to attain the realization of this unity with Brahman.

[17] *Brih Up*, IV, 4, 22.
[18] *RV*, I, 87, 4.
[19] *RV*, VIII, 17, 9.
[20] Cf. M. D. Shastri, 'History of the Word Isvara and Its Idea', in *Proc. and Trans. VII All-India Orient. Conf.*, Baroda, 1933, p. 487ff.
[21] *Svet Up*, III, 12.
[22] *Svet Up*, III, 16.
[23] Cf. *RV*, X, 72, 7.
[24] *Svet Up*, V, 3.
[25] *Kau Up*, III, 8.
[26] *Brih Up*, I, 4, 7.
[27] *Svet Up*, II, 15.

THE SPIRITUALITY OF THE UPANISHADS

The Upanishads propose a scheme of spiritual progress which is clearly distinct from its western equivalent. Even Christian spirituality, as developed in the West, is not an exception here, though it draws its substance from the Bible and the Hebrew approach to the godhead. Western spirituality starts from the supposition of the duality of God and the world of particular beings including human souls, and from that fact works towards a certain unity or union. The Upanishads take for granted the identity of all beings in the one Absolute Reality, and work for reaching a realization of this unity and identity in, through, and beyond the multiplicity of experience. The ideal proposed for man is to realize the Supreme Atman as his own self.

The Upanishads lead one to this realization through the six steps, indicated by the six *mahâvâkyâni* or the great statements :

1. *Ekamevam advitîyam,* One alone without a second : reality is One. Already, the *Rig Veda* had affirmed the absolute unity of all things in the Supreme, and the *Asyavamasya* hymn made the famous statement :

They call him Indra, Mitra, Varuna, Agni, and he is Garutman flying the heavens;
What is One, the wise men present in diverse ways as Agni, Yama and Matarisvan (*Rig Veda*, I, 164, 46).

What is One, the sages in their poetic conceptions present as many (*Rig Veda*, X, 114, 5; 129, 2). This basic unity of all things in the one absolute ground is the supposition against which the plurality of beings has to be evaluated. The Upanishadic quest is to attain this One beyond the many. That One is not additional to many. The many do not add anything to its infinite and immutable perfection.

2. *Neti, neti;* not so, not so : but, standing on this side of the many, bound in the world of plurality, we are not able to attain the Absolute. It is not possible to have experience of the One in and through the many. However, the relative reality of the world of experience has a pedagogical function in our search for the One. It tells us what the Absolute is not, and points the finger away from and beyond itself.

3. *Prajnânam Brahman* : *Brahman* is consciousness. Ultimate

Reality is consciousness. Even in the soul, what is of ultimate and permanent value is consciousness. So, only in and through consciousness can Supreme Consciousness be approached. The individual human, being bound by passions and ignorance, needs a certain purification to attain the realization of consciousness. This is a purification of finite, individual consciousness by the removal of the veil that hides the light within. Everything beside the light of consciousness is only a shadow. If the final goal of liberation is the removal of ignorance, it cannot be achieved by the acquisition and addition of concepts and images. A god, the Supreme Reality, who can be comprised in ideas and images, is no absolute at all, and therefore no god. The Supreme Reality is pure consciousness, limitless and immutable intelligence, beyond all conceptions and images. The only way to reach him is to remove the veils created by our mind; it is these which hide him.

4. *Atman Brahman* : the self and ground of each thing is God. The Supreme Reality should not be sought outside, as a thing among things, a person among persons. He is the ultimate ground that embraces all things. In the understanding of God, correlatives and contrasts, like inferior and superior, interior and exterior, one and many, cause and effect, etc., are totally irrelevant, for where one member of these opposites is God, they cannot be placed side by side. The world, as effect, cannot be contrasted with God as cause; the world does not add anything to the reality of God. The many do not deduct anything from the plenitude of the One. God is all, and nothing can add to him. He is the Atman, the self and total reality of all things.

5. *Aham Brahmâsmi* : my self is Brahman. Since God is everything, and since nothing can add to the reality of God, he cannot be known by contrast with others. The approach from our empirical self to God cannot be in the objective direction : divine reality is not a thing, nor a person among persons. God cannot strictly be placed in an I-Thou relationship with us, since our I-hood itself is only a reflexion of God's supra-personal reality. The only correct way of speaking about God is in the line of our own selfhood. Our self is the most unobjectifiable aspect of our being. It is the subject by which every object is known; hence it cannot become an object. Transcending every object, it is the symbol of God himself. God, who is the supreme subjectivity without the taint of objectness, can be understood only as the Self of our self, our real Self.

6. *Tattvamasi* : That art Thou. In relation with this Supreme Reality, the real *Tat*, everything else is a function. Even the *Guru*, the teacher, who utters this solemn liberating statement to the *sisya*, the disciple, is only a function of the divine, for concentrating and focusing all dissipated energies and aspirations of the aspirant. Even his individual selfhood, the finite *tvam*, Thou-hood, is only a function pointing to the Supreme Self. Hence, everything else besides the Supreme should be dealt with as a function in the spiritual endeavour, and never absolutized in opposition to God.

Functionalism in spiritual life

This functionalism is a cardinal point in the Hindu spiritual approach. Since the ideal of spiritual life is realization of God as the Supreme Reality and as the Self of one's own self, everything else is only a function of it, a means for attaining it, and is, therefore, valid only to the extent that it helps to bring about this realization.

Here, the concept of *adhikâra* is of great importance. Any ascetical practice or ritual and any of the particular *sâdhanas* and *upâdhis*, means and aids for spiritual life, can be helpful only for one who is particularly conditioned to profit from them. Thus, only one mentally conditioned by the conception of the *Saguna Brahman*, of God being in relation with the world, and only one who is desirous of enjoying the fruits, is the proper *adhikârin* to perform sacrifice and other rituals.[28]

Rita, the ideal of spiritual endeavour

The emphasis on *adhikâra* shows the real function of ascetical practices. Indian spirituality is not action-centred, as is Western spirituality. There is no attempt to remove impurities in order to reach the authentic. If the fact is recognized that all this multiplicity in our world of experience does not add anything to the absolute reality of God, nothing has to be purified, nothing has to be cut off. Only its position as a mere function in reference to God has to be recognized, its harmony with the Ultimate realized, and apparent conflicts resolved. These conflicts and complexities do not appear on the level of the divine transcendence, but only on the lower levels of our psychic experience. Hence, the particular line of a person's interests and aspirations will indicate the area of

[28] Cf. *Isa Up Sank Bh*, Introduction, and *Br S Sank Bh*, Introduction.

conflicts, and it is there that reconciliation has to be effected, and on that plane that tranquillity has to be sought.

In Indian spiritual thought, *sânti* is the highest spiritual attainment, because in it all psychic levels are transcended and all conflicts resolved in a full possession of God, the Self of our self. It is a supra-conceptual apprehension of the Absolute, on the one hand, and a supra-mental experience of cosmic unity, on the other. In reference to this ideal state, even a positive attitude to the world of beings is stated in negative terms. Thus, *Ahimsa,* non-violence, implies not only avoidance of all violence, but also practice of benevolence and friendship. Sentimental reaction to the world around us is designated by the negative term *akrodha,* which means not only the avoidance of anger, but also the positive exercise of all virtues of the heart. *Adroha* is not merely desisting from causing harm to others, but also rendering them all positive help. But all these belong to the relative world of our existence and are therefore stated in negative terms.

Organization of ascetical life

A spiritual life which emphasizes the post-reflexive, supra-conceptual and supra-mental realization of the Supreme for ideal should, at the same time, ascribe equal importance to *artha,* wealth, *kâma,* pleasure, *dharma,* righteousness, and *môksha,* liberation. This may look rather paradoxical. The reason for this accent on the four goals of life is that spirituality is not life-negating, but life-affirming. On each level of life, in each field of its activity, harmony and tranquillity have to be established by eliminating all dissipation, and emphasizing the proper function of each factor.

Tapas, or austerities, are needed to control and organize the psychic forces, but they are not a purgation, nor an inhibition, and much less a mortification. As the word *tapas* implies, it is the intensification of spiritual energy in its proper centre, Brahman. It orientates all one's powers to the ultimate and supreme goal.

Sraddhâ, or faith, is also an essential requisite for spiritual progress, but it is not merely an intellectual assent to a divinely enunciated proposition, nor a leap in the dark in blind credulity. It is, first and foremost, a judgment of the functionality of the finite world, by which one surrenders all that one is and all that one has to the Supreme Lord.

Upâsanâ, or meditation, is one of the principal means to attain tranquillity of spirit. However, it is not merely an exercise of the imagination and of the intellect by which principles are analyzed and understood, conclusions drawn and practical programmes in life mapped out. Its scope is to go deep within oneself and find the link between the psychic forces and cosmic powers, not merely to find a parallelism between the two, but to realize how the two constitute two aspects of the same harmony. For this, one has to start with one's own biological or mental experiences and strive to realize their ultimate ground.[29]

In this endeavour, everything becomes a function. The *pancâgni-vidyâ*, or the meditation on the five fires,[30] is particularly illustrative of this method of approach. The fifth and lowest fire is a wife, allied with childbirth and family cares, which one offers up and sublimates in a mental sacrifice. This process of sublimation proceeds upwards through the levels of food, rain and moon until *sraddhâ*, faith, is reached. This last one is a heavenly fire that is poured out as a final oblation.

Upâsanâ need not necessarily be a concentration on God. It is not for the sake of God, but for man; besides, human concentration can never reach God as he is in his intimate reality. Hence, according to Sankara, *abrahmopâsanâ* is equally useful as *brahmo-pâsanâ*, because its function is to go beyond the conventional identi-fication between one's self and one's body and individuality, which is the source of all conflicts and disharmonies. Through concentra-tion, one strives to go beyond oneself and to get identified with the transcendental, with the same intensity as that of one's identity with the body.[31] This means that material things are used in spiritual endeavour, not as means and techniques, but rather as a path, a way, a function. Spiritual life is the path to self-fulfilment and salvation, and not a set of techniques for producing anything. Anything produced is transitory. Life attains unity and stability in its union with its ultimate ground, Brahman.

SPECIFIC CHARACTERISTICS OF HINDU PHILOSOPHY

The world vision of the Upanishads, briefly explained above, presents certain specific characteristics which constitute the identity of Indian tradition itself.

[29] Cf. *Prâna Upâsanâ* in *Pras Up*, II, and *Manopâsanâ* in *Tait Up*, III, 1–6.

[30] *Brih Up*, VI, 2; *Chând Up*, V, 4–10.

[31] *Brih Up Sank Bh*, I, 3, 9.

(1) The reason for this identity is first of all historical and geographical. Indian thought evolved in a geographical situation of natural plenty, in which man had to concern himself very little about his material needs. Even up to the last century, the natural wealth of India held the greatest fascination for traders and invaders. Hence, philosophy did not occupy itself with organizing the material world or with the setting up of political kingdoms (except at a later stage), but was concerned mainly with the spiritual problems of man, his ignorance and suffering, old age and death.

(2) For the same reason, Indian thought focused itself on human life. This created an intimate relationship between philosophical speculation and practical life.

(3) This concentration on human life explains the special philosophical method adopted in Indian tradition. Human life cannot properly be understood except by self-examination. Hence, the conscious self became the focal point of all philosophical investigations, in the place of the objective reality taken as a point of departure by western thought.

(4) Western tradition realistically had to take for granted the multiplicity of things and seek to discover a principle of unity among them. Indian thinkers, however, did not find unity a problem. Man, living in favourable natural surroundings, spontaneously feels himself at home with the whole creation. Unity is a given fact for him. Ignorance and suffering, disturbance and disunity, and multiplicity itself, look anomalous to him. Hence, multiplicity was the problem which demanded to be reconciled with the unity that was taken for granted. This unity, admitted as the starting point by all the schools of Indian philosophy, is not an organic or structural co-existence of factors, but the absolute and ultimate oneness of all things in one infinite reality.

(5) This supposition of ultimate unity meant that solutions to problems did not have to be created afresh or discovered by reasoning. They were already there in the fundamental and authentic unity of things. Hence, the method of procedure was not one of analytical investigation or objective reasoning, but *anubhava*, realization, the becoming conscious of the One that already was there in the many.

(6) On account of the inadequacy of finite reason to reach reality all by itself, tradition and authority have a special place of importance in Indian philosophy. Scripture is the written record of

the realization of the sages concerning the Ultimate Reality. Though the written word as such is not absolute, it nevertheless helps one towards having the same realization of which it is the record much better than any independent investigation.

(7) Above all, an integral approach is the dominant characteristic of Indian thought. Since immediate realization of the Absolute Reality is seen as the final goal of the inquiry, every view and every particular theory is considered in the total context, a partial and inadequate opinion but, all the same, contributing something to the final knowledge. Hence, no positive element of thought, however imperfect, can be rejected. This is the basic principle underlying the attitude of tolerance : every view and theory and opinion should be respected for the element of truth encased in it.

Such was the philosophical outlook which shaped Hinduism as a religion.

CHAPTER VIII

SYSTEMATIC DEVELOPMENT OF HINDU PHILOSOPHY

Hindu philosophy is not the development of a single line of thought. It shows the tensions, complexities and compromises of a number of thought-currents which came eventually to form a single unified tradition. These tensions were kept alive down the ages by the systematic schools which represented one or other of the thought-trends. These schools were divided into six main systems, roughly aligned to different philosophical problems: namely, *Vaiseshika*, cosmology; *Nyâya*, logic; *Sâmkhya*, psychology; *Yoga*, asceticism; *Mîmâmsa*, ritual; and *Vedânta*, metaphysics.

This division is definitely artificial and is employed mostly for pedagogical reasons. Problems discussed by these schools do overlap. Still, taken cumulatively, they represent a converging inward movement which strives to attain the one Ultimate Reality. Thus, *Vaiseshika* strives to understand all reality in terms of physical categories of substance, action, quality, relation, and the rest, representing the external experience of man; *Nyâya*, on the other hand, stands for the thought of man endeavouring to match external experience with his logical divisions and subdivisions.

Both *Sâmkhya* and *Yoga* deal with reality in psychological categories, but the former with a cosmic vision of the matter-spirit duality, and the latter with a view to transcending the duality within one's own self.

Mîmâmsa and *Vedânta* deal with reality as such, but the former takes reality in its non-physical aspect of the word, which embraces everything and yet stands in a way detached from all physical existence. *Vedânta*, on the other hand, interiorized even the word itself in its pure transcendental aspects, realized fully in the one ultimate self.

For the sake of brevity, we shall deal with the philosophy presented in these systems at these three levels: logic, psychology, and metaphysics. This will help us to present the positive contribution of Hindu thought as a multi-layered philosophical view of reality.

EXPERIENCE, LOGIC AND REALITY

Predominance of logic at a given period of history is often taken for a sign of decadence. After a period of intense activity in search of reality, there comes a lull when people take stock of their achievements and methods of procedure and discuss even the very method of discussion. The Sophists and the later Academicians mark such transitional periods in Greek philosophy. After the golden age of Scholasticism in the later Middle Ages, there is a long period when Nominalism and Conceptualism seem to dominate all philosophy. In Indian tradition, too, after the creative period of the Upanishads, there was a period when *nyâya*, logic and argumentation, emerged as the principal concern in philosophy. Again, after the most productive period starting with Sankara and closing with Ramanuja in the 12th century of the Christian era, there was a resurgence of logic under the name of *Navya Nyâya*, new logic, which gave the pride of place to scholastic disputation. These periods were a preparation for new lines of investigation; they also provided their own particular insights into the nature of reality.

Historical Evolution : The beginnings of a science of logic are found early in Indian tradition. Logic is designated by several Sanskrit terms, *hetu vidya* or *hetusâstra*, science of causes, *anvîksiki*, scence of inquiry, *pramânasâstra*, science of the means of correct knowledge, *tattvasâstra*, science of categories, *tarkavidya* or *vâd-ârtha*, the art of disputation, *pakkikasâstra*, science of sophism, and especially *nyâya*. The grammarian Panini derives the term *nyâya* from the root 'i', go, with the sense of leading one from the premises to the conclusion in a syllogism.[1] *Nyâya* was already a well-developed science at the time of the spread of Buddhism. *Brahmajala Sutta* and *Udâna* of the Pali canon speak of the Samanas and Brahmanas who were *takki* or *takkikas* and *vimâmsis*, logicians and casuists. The Pali canon mentions also a group called Gotamakas, probably followers of Gautama, the author of the *Nyâya Sûtras*.[2]

That in the beginning there was a certain amount of resistance

[1] *Panini*, III, 3, 122.
[2] *Manu Smriti*, II, 11.

to the use of reasoning and argumentation in religious beliefs is easily understandable. Thus, Manu, the legislator, enjoins that those Brahmins who relied so much on *hetusâstra* as to neglect the Vedas should be excluded from the class of the sages.[3] *Ramayana* calls those who apply logic to religion, especially to *dharmasâstra*, moral doctrine, perverse.[4] The *Santiparvam* of the *Mahabharata* relates the conversation between Kasyapa, a Brahmin, and Indra, in the form of a jackal: Indra tells the Brahmin that he was condemned to the form of the jackal on account of his attachment, for the purpose of vain disputations, to logic and its application to the Vedas.[5] It prohibits the communication of religious doctrine to mere logicians.[6] However, right reasoning itself is not excluded from the study of *dharma*.[7] Logic is one of the necessary sciences prescribed for the education of kings.[8] It is counted as one of the fourteen principal sciences.[9] Its origin is ascribed, along with the Vedas, to the mouth of Brahma himself.[10]

The *Nyâya Sûtras* of Gautama is the earliest extant work on logic. This work is dated around 4th or 5th century B.C., but it has several sections which are clearly of a later date. It has been commented upon by a great many teachers of the school, among whom Vatsayana (A.D. 450), Udyotakara, Vacaspati Misra (9th cent. A.D.), Bhawarvajna, Jayanta and Udayana (10th cent.) are prominent.

Approach to Reality from Logical Categories: The *Nyâya* system attempts to reach reality through a rational analysis of knowledge. It shows that knowledge is not a simple formless awareness, but a complex phenomenon, both on account of the different operations involved in a single act of reasoning, and of the different faculties of man involved in the act of knowing.

No single piece of knowledge is gained by a direct intuition. One has to concentrate on an object of knowledge, fix the purpose of knowing, and also employ certain definite means for attaining right knowledge. Several possibilities of a case have to be weighed, similar cases recalled, various steps in one's own procedure checked,

[3] *Ramayana,* Ayodhyakanda, 100.
[4] *Mahabharata,* Santiparvam, Ch. 180, 47–9.
[5] *Ibid.,* Ch. 246, 18.
[6] *Manu Smriti,* XII, 106.
[7] *Yajnavalkhyasamhita,* I, 3.
[8] *Manu Smriti,* VII, 43; XII, 111.
[9] *Matsyapurana,* III, 2.
[10] *Mahabharata,* Adiparvam, Chs. 1 and 70.

opposite views and arguments excluded, and finally a definite conclusion arrived at. Only in this way can man attain his final happiness which is in the line of knowledge; bondage is ignorance. On the whole, *Nyâya* advocates a common-sense approach in the quest for the Ultimate Reality.

According to Vatsayana, *anvîkshi*, or logical reflexion, has a definite place in the realization of human goals in life. It leads man to liberation from worldly existence which is the final objective of life. Of the three other aims of life, worldly prosperity and wealth are attained through *vartta*, or the vocational science dealing with agriculture, trade, etc.; *kâma*, or pleasure, through the enjoyment of the amenities of life is made possible through *dandaniti*, or polity which controls passions, desires, and emotions and provides for social welfare. Even religious life as presented in the *Trayi*, the three Vedas (*Rig, Yajus* and *Sama*), organizes human life only within the structure of this worldly existence through *dharma*, or duty. *Nyâya* goes beyond all these three by aiming at the transcendental values of reality and existence.

In dealing with liberation, there is the question of a kind of knowledge which is not yet attained. *Nyâya*, or reasoning according to the proponents of the *Nyâya* system, has no function where the object is already attained and ascertained, and also where the object is totally unperceived or absolutely unattainable. It has scope only where one has already some idea of the object, but has not realized it fully, and is therefore in a state of doubt or hesitation. The final ascertainment is 'the determination of the object by means of opposite views after a first impression'.[11] The order of procedure to this final realization has to be conceived according to the progression of logical thought: a first impression, doubt, opposite views, application of reasoning, determination of the object, ascertainment through reflexion, and final certitude. For the *Nyâya* school, this logical procedure of thought represents man's ontological advance to his final goal.

Samsaya or *Doubt*: Doubt is one of the basic categories for the *Nyâya* school, but it is not mere absence of knowledge, not even a theoretical questioning, nor hesitation between two alternatives. It stands for man's first step towards the realization of his ultimate goal, the first impression and indeterminate knowledge of the ultimate reality. Here, *prayôjanâ*, or purpose, both of the human life

[11] *Ny S*, I, i, 41.

as a whole and of the logical activity in particular, is the moving force. It is the goal one wants to attain, be it either the object one desires to obtain, or the evil one strives to avoid. Purpose pervades all things, motivates all actions, gives meaning to the whole world of reality.

Nyâya or *Reasoning* : Reasoning itself has several principal members : proposition, reason, example, applications and conclusion. Proposition is an initial statement concerning the object, forecasting what it will be. There are two kinds of forecasts, the initial, vague and indeterminate knowledge (*nirvikalpa pratyaksha*) and the later, reflective, direct knowledge specified by genus and name (*savikalpaka pratyaksha*).[12] More important is the distinction between the affirmative knowledge of something and its realization : every reasoning starts with a statement, an affirmation of what is to be proved. This affirmation corresponds to the indeterminate knowledge one gets about a thing from a certain distance. Affirmation admits the existence of what is affirmed. The affirmed is totally other, opposed to and distinct from the mind. Hence, there is no intimate relation between it and the one who affirms it. Mere affirmation does not provide meaningful knowledge about the affirmed. Thus, the affirmation of the ultimate good does not guarantee any actual understanding of the ultimate real.

In fact, affirmation and realization proceed in opposite directions : what is affirmed is constituted in a sphere distinct from, and opposed to, the affirming mind. Realization, on the other hand, strives to achieve a certain unity and identity between the two. *Hetu*, reason, *udâharana*, example and *upanaya*, application, bring about this rapprochement between the knower and the known. *Hetu*, reason (or the Middle Term), is the better known which leads to a better understanding of the less known. Example, or analogy, in some manner brings down the unknown object to the field of the everyday experience of the knower. Application declares that the object affirmed pertains to the very cognitive horizon of the knower.

Hence, the members of the *Nyâya* reasoning are not mere explanatory additions to an ordinary deductive syllogism. Syllogism is strictly an elaboration of the affirmation, bringing out what is already implied in the affirmation of the major and minor terms

---

[12] This distinction was probably introduced later by the Mîmâmsaka logicians like Kumarila Bhatta, but it is read back into the *Sûtras* (I, i, 4) by Vacaspati Misra.

with reference to a common middle term. All the three terms remain in the objective field, opposed to and independent of the knowing subject. There, the principal effort is to interrelate the general and the particular, the universal and the concrete. The *Nyâya* school, on the other hand, primarily tries to relate what is stated as the object of inquiry to the familiar field of the knowing subject. Not merely the interrelation between several objects is explored, but their relevance to the understanding subject as well. In this perspective, example or analogy has a special significance, since it brings the matter of investigation to the familiarity of daily experience while, in a purely objective examination, example is not a strictly valid argument, since no two cases are absolutely identical.

Tarka, Vâda, Jalpa and Vitanda : In putting the object of knowledge in concrete relationship with the knowing subject, it is necessary to view it in as many relations as possible with human life. In this relating of objects with life, counter-opinions, objections and disputations have great importance. *Vâda* or assertion, and *Jalpa*, sophistry, by proposing opposing views and specious counter-arguments, place the truth in contrasting perspective. Even *vitanda*, which is destructive (and often irrelevant) criticism of a certain point of view, is useful, since it calls for a vigorous defence of a proposed position. *Tarka*, or hypothesis, has the function of bringing out various side-aspects of an apparently simple issue.

The conclusion of such a laborious and complex procedure is fittingly called *nigamana*, an arriving at, reaching the end of a long journey led by reason. Knowledge is no simple intuition, no speculative theory cut away from concrete reality, but a personal intimacy with truth. The concept of *parâmarsa* developed by Udyotakara, a later *Nyâya* philosopher, further emphasizes this intimacy of relation in knowledge : it is the discovery in a new thing of an already familiar aspect. Arriving at a conclusion in reasoning supposes two prior steps : first, the cognition of the relation between a certain distinguishing note in reference to a general category of object, and second, the discovery of the same mark in a concrete particular object. Every *nigamana*, conclusion, is a rediscovery.

THE PRAMANAS—MEANS OF RIGHT KNOWLEDGE

The affirmative and objective approach tries to reduce all objective reality to the subject-predicate pattern, with the 'is' serving as a mere connecting link. Modern logic has emphasized the fact that the complex structure of the objective world—consisting of substance, quality, action and relation—cannot be reduced to this oversimplified form. Symbolic logic has tried to provide tools for representing a great variety of relationships in the objective world. *Nyâya*, which had in view the complex relationships in concrete life, did not restrict itself to a mere subject-predicate pattern. For it, the complex ways in which knowledge related the mind to things were themselves the primary patterns for reality. Hence, it laid the greatest emphasis on *pramânas*, or means of right knowledge. All the other schools of Hindu thought share this special concern with the means of right knowledge, though they differ on the number of *pramânas* they recognize.

The means of right knowledge recognized by *Nyâya* are perception (*pratyaksha*), inference (*anumâna*), comparison (*upamâna*), and word or verbal testimony (*sabda*). *Nyâya* takes a common-sense view of knowledge. It considers knowledge as the subject's relation to the world of objects. It is not a quality of the object known, but 'a light that abides in the self and makes things understood'. Gautama identified cognition (*buddhi*) with knowledge (*jnâna*) and apprehension (*upalabdhi*).[13] The commentator Prasastapada added to these comprehension (*pratyaya*) as implied in knowledge.[14] This knowledge is a union of the subject with things; not a merely passive impression from them, but an active illumination of them.

Hence, a direct contact with things (*vastupagama*) is the ultimate and final criterion for our acceptance of reality.[15] *Pratyaksha*, or direct perception, comes as the most immediate union with reality. This is true in sense experience as well as in spiritual realization. In *yogipratyaksha*, or yogic vision, the ultimate reality is intuited without the aid of any sensible images. In ordinary experience, too, the senses are directly joined (*samyoga*) to their special objects. In inference, analogy, and verbal testimony, mind's union with objects is diversely remote and mediate. In this connection, it may be recalled that *Nyâya* proposes some six different kinds of union: simple conjunction (*samyoga*), inherence in the conjoint (*samyukta samavâya*), simple inherence (*samavâya*), inherence in the inherent

[13] *Ny S*, I, i, 15.
[14] Cf. A. B. Keith, *Indian Logic and Atomism* (Oxford: Clarendon Press, 1921), pp. 42–9.
[15] Vacaspati Misra, *Nyâyâvârtikatâtparyatîka* (Calcutta, 1898), p. 506.

in the conjoint (*samyukta samaveta samavâya*), inherence in the inherent (*samaveta samavâya*) and simple relation of subject and predicate (*viseshyaviseshana*).

Knowledge of Non-Existence : Throughout the long history of Indian thought, the concept of non-existence had a central place in Indian philosophy, especially since the Buddhist school emphasized the negation of all limited and conceivable existence. Mîmâmsakas postulated a special *pramâna*, a valid means of knowing non-existence : valid non-perception. When I look into Peter's room and say, 'Peter is not there', I am reporting my non-perception of Peter where he was expected to be. But the *Nyâya* school rightly argues that the negative aspect—for example, the absence of Peter —is perceived by the same means by which the positive is apprehended : it is the perception of the room got ready for Peter, *minus* Peter. Hindu schools distinguish four kinds of non-existence : prior, consequent, mutual and absolute. From the sight of a flash of lightning, one understands its prior non-existence, and from the same vision, also, its consequent non-existence after it has disappeared. Contrary concepts imply mutual non-existence; light means the non-existence of darkness and *vice versa*. Absolute non-existence is the negation of everything positive : this is the case of impossibility. You cannot find a pot where there is no pot.

The particular philosophical outlook of Indian tradition makes non-existence a very important concept. Hindu thought is not pre-occupied with the origin of things or their future condition. It is first and foremost concerned about what they actually are. What they actually and essentially are is what they were, and what they will always be. The essential in a thing is what is immutable; a cow is essentially a cow and it cannot but be a cow. Non-existence in any form argues the unreality and transitoriness of the thing involved. Hence, non-existence is the condition of time-bound existence. *Nyâya-Vaiseshika* schools defend *asatkâryavâda*, the theory of prior non-existence in causality. According to them, prior non-existence is the normal condition of anything caused. Anything caused is not its own self; it is new; it came into existence. To conceive a prior subtle state in which the new thing existed is to deny its newness and causality itself. Anything caused comes out of its prior non-existence. Similarly, when something has ceased to exist, there is consequent non-existence. To imagine a subtle state in which the thing which ceased to exist continues to exist is a contradiction in terms. The prior and consequent states of a conceivable thing are not conceivable. Negation should be the principal method in the investigation of the reality of a transitory thing. Deny all you can; you will deny only what is conceivable. Prior and consequent non-existence are inconceivable. So also is the true condition of the cause.

Language and Meaning: This concern with the true state of things, instead of their transitory aspects, gave *Nyâya* logic a certain detachment from experience with an added emphasis on the meaning of concepts and statements. The meaning-function of knowledge was enunciated in the classical statement: *Arthaprakâso buddhi. Buddhi* means both intellect and its act of cognition. Its function is to reveal *artha. Artha*, in its original meaning, indicated objects or goal of action, but it later came more and more to indicate the 'meaning' of words and statements. In this sense, the statement would mean that the function of knowledge is to reveal meaning.

According to the school of the Grammarians, only a sentence has meaning. But the Naiyayikas ascribed meaning to words also. Nevertheless, for them, too, a *vâkya*, or sentence, has a meaning distinct from that of the words constituting it being simply put together. Hence, an important problem was to decide what constituted a sentence. A number of definitions were attempted. Some of them were:

— A sentence is an indivisible unit of letters and words suggesting a meaning.
— A *vâkya*, or statement, which may be taken as being identical with knowledge.
— Only that knowledge which suggests the combination of qualities, substances, actions and relations constitutes a sentence.
— Any body of words which can produce meaning is a sentence.
— Only a body of words which appear in a definite order, and appear as members of one another, can constitute a sentence.[16]

But Jaimini, the reputed author of the *Mîmâmsa Sûtras*, gives the most comprehensive definition: *arthaikatvadekam vâkyam sakamksakam vibhaga syat*: a statement or sentence is a combination of words, internally coherent and suggesting a single meaning, if analysis is made.[17] It is interesting to note how these various defini-

[16] Sri Ramanuja, *Commentary on the Nyâyaratnamâla of Parthasarathi-misra* (Baroda, 1937), p. 89.
[17] *Mîmâmsa Sûtras*, II, i, 46.

tions insist on the main points of syntactic unity and meaning: definite order of words, internal coherence, singleness of meaning and, above all, reference to an order of reality consisting of substance, qualities, actions and relations.

There is the further question as to how a plurality of words can give a single meaning, even when the physical elements of sound have died out. Grammarians like Bhartrihari and Patanjali distinguish, in a statement, the *prakritadhwani*, or individual voice of the speaker, the *vyakritadhwani*, or general import of the words, and an invisible, spiritual unitary element, *sphota*, contained in each statement. This *sphota* is the meaning unit communicated to the listeners.

The Naiyayikas reject this invisible entity. They also oppose the belief of the Mîmâmsakas that only the universal and not the individual is known. Against both these positions, *Nyâya* held that a sentence or statement is a linguistic utterance and is a collection of sounds produced by the movements of the vocal organs of the speaker, and are by their very nature ephemeral. The recognition of letters and words uttered by different persons at different times is explained by the fact that they are particular instances of the same universal. The idea of identity is created by their similarity. Similarly, according to *Nyâya*, both *jâti* and *vyakti*, the universal and the particular, are perceived in the same thing. An individual is indicated and referred to by the universal note, and the universal note is present in individuals.

KNOWLEDGE AND TRUTH

For Indian philosophers in general, the problem of meaning is more complex than that of truth. The intimate relation between consciousness or knowledge and reality makes any simple correspondence or intuition theories look too naive in the light of Indian philosophical tradition. Knowledge itself implies a good many syntheses on different planes, where all the various correspondences can be examined. In affirming something, there is first of all a logical synthesis between two concepts represented by the subject and predicate in a sentence. Besides this, there is a predicative synthesis between the knowing subject and the particular object that is affirmed, a subjective synthesis between the activities of the senses and of the intellect within the same knowing subject, an objective synthesis within the object between its sensible qualities and intelligible reality. What is more fundamental than all these is the ultimate reality and truth in reference to which this particular knowledge has relevance and meaning.

In this last respect—in reference to absolute reality—truth is only a function of knowledge : a particular knowledge is true in as much as it leads to and/or shares in an ultimate truth. However, this truth function is conceived differently by different schools, according to the difference in the conception of truth itself. For the *Sâmkhya-Yoga* schools, knowledge is a self-contained mechanical process of reflecting things in the mirror of *buddhi*, a manifestation of the potentialities of *Prakriti*, and therefore did not need any correspondence to the things of the external world for its truth. Several Vedânta scholars defend the *svayamprakâsatva*, self-luminosity of knowledge, and so do not require any further illumination for its truth. It is self-evident. The Mîmâmsakas hold that there is a certain parallelism between our knowledge and things outside but, according to them, things do not cause our knowledge, but rather knowledge makes things known. They, too, therefore, defend the self-evidence of knowledge, and consider truth an intrinsic aspect of it.[18]

For the Naiyayikas, however, truth is a super-added function. Knowledge is an attribute produced in the self through some extrinsic cause. By itself, it does not require either to be in accord or in discord with the object to which it is supposed to refer. Its conformity or disagreement with things is something extrinsic to it and, hence, has to be ascertained through other means. The reason for this *Nyâya* position with regard to the truth value of our knowledge is that the *Nyâya-Vaiseshika* categories are just a metaphysical classification of all knowable objects or of all real, a mere enumeration of the different states of things, real or possible.[19] Hence, their truth or actual verification in the real order is something super-added to them. As A. B. Keith says : according to *Nyâya*, 'each cognition is true in virtue of a quality (*guna*) which it possesses, and is false in virtue of a defect (*dosha*); or, more simply, a cognition is true or false in so far as it fulfils or fails to fulfil some requisite.[20]

[18] A. B. Keith, *op. cit.*, p. 46.
[19] Chandradhar Sharma, *A Critical Survey of Indian Philosophy*, p. 176.
[20] A. B. Keith, *op. cit.*, pp. 55–6.

Truth and Error: This difference in the conception of truth is particularly clear in the various theories on error. Error is not a mere lack of correspondence. It is judged in terms of the ultimate meaning of truth. What lacks that ultimate meaning is error. Thus, the Yogâcâra school of Buddhism, which conceived all conditioned existence as mere mental conception, and that, too, illusory, defends the *âtma-khyâti* theory about error: every error is self-projection, a concept which exists only because the mind wrongly appears as a thing in the external world. The Madhyamika school of Buddhism, which proceeds by negating all conditioned existence—and all existence is conditioned—is the proponent of *asat-khyâti* theory: in an erroneous perception, an unreal thing, *e.g.*, a piece of silver, appears as real, although it is only a piece of shell. Those, like Sankara, who hold that the Absolute alone is real, propose the *anirvacanîya khyâti* as an explanation for error: the object of an erroneous perception is not real; nor is it mere non-existence. It is undefinable either as real or as unreal. The opposite of true is not false, but non-true, the opposite of real is not unreal, but non-real (*a-n-rita*); the opposite side of true knowledge is not ignorance, but non-knowledge (*avidyâ*). For the Mîmâmsakas, according to their parallelism between mental forms and things, error is *akhyâti*, illusion, in which the distinction between that which really exists and that which is cognized is not perceived. Illusion is partly remembrance and partly apprehension; illusory perception also appears to be true and valid as a correct perception.

Against these schools, *Nyâya* proposes the theory of *anyathâ-khyâti* or *viparîtakhyâti*; wrong cognition consists in mistaking one thing for another. The peculiar qualities of the object which actually exist are not clearly noticed. Attention is concentrated on the general qualities, and so one thing is perceived for another on account of the common general characteristics. In every error there is not only the failure to perceive the particular distinguishing characteristics of the thing, but also a positive false identification of one thing with another. This may be owing to the obscurity of the thing itself, or the defect of the senses, or the lack of proper attention.

CONCLUSION

From what has been explained above, it may appear that the preoccupations of ancient Hindu logicians were identical with those of contemporary logic. It is true that contemporary logical problems were not totally unknown to the ancients.

(1) They were struggling to define the various relationships in which things were apprehended in knowledge. Human knowledge and logic are meaningful only in as much as they refer to facts.

(2) The meaningful unit of knowledge is not a mere idea, but a word or statement in which the internal consistency refers to a possible external order of things.

(3) Thought and language do not fall into the simple subject-predicate pattern, but follow different patterns of complex combinations.

(4) Truth is not the intrinsic characteristic of thought and logic, but only incidental to them, through correspondence to facts. Truth is only a function of knowledge.

(5) Empirical verification can be taken as the ultimate test of the validity of knowledge and language. But this experience should not be considered in its sensory momentariness, but rather in the total context, both from the aspect of objective totality and from that of subjective synthesis between sense and intellect.

But these logical problems are not the major concern for Hindu logicians. For them, logic is essentially theology, the necessary means for indicating to the soul the path for self-realization. Even when developing subtle methodological systems, the Hindu thinker is concerned with the ultimate and ineffable reality. Man at present is in a state of bondage. Bondage is essentially error and ignorance and the lack of right knowledge. Hence, the elaborate discussion of logical problems is basically the inquiry into the ultimate felicity of man.

CHAPTER IX

PSYCHOLOGY AND PERSONALITY

A dark spot in Greek philosophical tradition is the lack of proper emphasis on the human person. Person was considered a thing among other things, very much as a concrete, intellectual substance. In contrast, a characteristic feature of Hindu philosophy is the importance attached to the concept of the person right from the beginning. The *Rig Veda* extols the cosmic person, from whom the whole universe of beings is said to have emerged. The Sâmkhya-Yoga schools present the psychological context for a metaphysics of the person.

These schools provide a metaphysical framework for a discussion of personality as the ground of all reality, though *Yoga* places the emphasis on the ascetical scheme, according to which the person can attain his own authentic reality and ultimate perfection. The origins of the Sâmkhya school are not quite clear. It is often considered to be a system built on to the Vedic tradition by the absorption and assimilation of non-Aryan traditions, rather than one emerging directly from the Vedas.[1] The earliest extant text-book of the Sâmkhya school is the *Sâmkhya Kârikâ*, ascribed to Iswara Krishna. The *Sâmkhya Sûtras*, though often ascribed to Kapila, the reputed Father of the Sâmkhya school, probably dates from the 15th century A.D. *Sâmkhya Kârikâ*, with the commentaries of Gaudapada, Vacaspati Misra,[2] and other later teachers of the school, gives us a fair idea of the philosophical line of thought represented by the school.

---

[1] A. B. Keith, *Sâmkhya System* (Calcutta: YMCA Publishing House, 2nd ed., 1949), pp. 7–9. Sri Sankaracharya argues against the authoritativeness of the Sâmkhya system, for it contradicts the Veda (*Ved S Sank Bh,* II, 1, 2–3, Sacred Books of the East, Vol. XXXIV, pp. 295, 297–8).

[2] Cf. *Sâm K of Iswara Krishna* with *Gaudapada Bhâshya,* ed. T. G. Mainkar (Poona: Oriental Book Agency, 1964); *The Tattva Kaumudi, Vacaspati Misra's Commentary on the Sâm K,* trs. Ganganath Jha, ed. Har Dutt Sharma and M. M. Patkar (Poona: Oriental Book Agency, 1965).

SUFFERING, THE STARTING POINT OF PHILOSOPHY

The first statement of the *Sâmkhya Kârikâ* sets forth suffering as the starting point of inquiry : 'On account of affliction from three-fold misery, inquiry should be instituted into the means for its removal.'[3] The nature of misery and the means for its avoidance cannot be taken for granted as evident, since ordinary knowledge about them lacks certainty and finality. According to Plato, philosophy starts with wonder. The Greek detached or objective outlook on the world of experience, suggested by the presence of the strange and anomalous, initiated an impartial examination of the entities presented in experience. For the Indian tradition, however, philosophizing is not an idle pastime, but the urgent need of the human spirit beset with pain and misery. The anomaly is not outside, but deep within man himself. Ignorance, suffering and death cannot be accepted as normal conditions. Hence, the inquiry should go beyond the field of misery to the authentic reality, as well as to the nature of the means that will remove suffering.[4]

Suffering places man at the cross-roads of phenomenal reality. His suffering comes from three sources : from interior causes, both bodily and mental; from external understandable and often controllable agents like men and beasts; or from forces beyond his comprehension and control, such as the natural phenomena of heat and cold, storm, rain and thunderbolt. All these are under the auspices of the divine powers. These three categories require different approaches for their proper understanding. Man's internal suffering and its causes can be understood by internal experience and introspection. External causes fall within the experience of the senses. Things which come from a divine source have to be understood by recourse to scripture and the teaching of the sages.

The main point here is that mere experience alone will not give a full and satisfactory explanation. It lacks certainty (*ekântatah*) and finality (*atyantatah*).[5] All that experience can do is to explain multiplicity in terms of the multiple factors, and account for ignorance by pointing out the structure of imperfect knowledge. Even the

---

[3] *Sâm K,* Kârikâ 1.

[4] Vacaspati Misra, in his commentary on the first Kârikâ, says that expositions on problems which do not affect the life of the people directly cannot interest them. People only understand doctrines which lead to the attainment of the highest aims of man (*loc. cit.,* p. 2).

[5] *Gaudapada Bhâshya on Kârikâ I,* pp. 2–3.

message of scripture is presented in forms and categories tainted with multiplicity and change. Nevertheless, stability is better than change, consciousness better than mere entity, unity better than multiplicity. Hence, any true explanation should go beyond the field of experience to the level of pure consciousness—consciousness which is free from change, individuality and duality. This alone can provide absolute certainty.

Similarly, a solution to the problem of suffering should have finality. As long as some uncalculated eventuality is left for the emergence of misery, man's life is not secure. As long as he remains open to the impact of the three levels of being—internal multiplicity, external enemies, and unaccountable and uncontrollable supernal forces—he is liable to suffer as a victim of those influences. Hence, to stand firm against these forces, man has to find his ultimate ground and self-identity beyond the reach of these forces of multiplicity.

In searching for this ultimate ground and self of man, Indian tradition takes for granted the ultimate unity of all reality and absolute purity of the Self as facts, and rarely takes pains to explain and prove this basic supposition. Multiplicity, change and ignorance are anomalies and exceptions to these basic facts. A certain transcendence of the Self over all the multiplicity of experience is the horizon or projected solution towards which the whole investigation is directed, and so the authentic and pure Self is both the starting point and goal of the philosophical journey.

The Phenomenon of Experience

For all this, the Sâmkhya-Yoga school does not ignore or bypass the world of experience, which is a world of multiplicity. The whole inquiry is located in experience itself, so that it may be transcended through its own dynamism. Experience shows man as a dynamic centre of the whole structure of things, actions, feelings, qualities and states that constitute the world of our individual existence.

This complex structure, manifested in experience, can be approached from several angles in order to explore the authentic and immutable in it. It can be examined in its objective and entitative reality and examined for its ultimate causes, or considered purely in the phenomenological aspect, placing the emphasis on its coherent structure as presented in our conscious experience, or dealt with in its conscious significance as it points away from its own individual structure. Of these, Indian tradition places the accent on the third approach.

Objective and causal approach

An objective and causal approach can deal with the human self as a thing like any other thing, and distinguish the substance from the accidents in it, the act of existence from the essence, and the principle of actuality, unity and finality from its co-principle of limitation and receptivity. This conception makes a clear and irreducible distinction between the spiritual soul in man and his material body, the soul and its faculties, the universal nature of man and the individual human being, who alone is a person. A person in this outlook will be a distinct and subsistent entity with an intellectual nature.

The drawback of this approach is that it objectifies the subject and makes the self a thing among other things. The subject is that which is opposed to the object and knows it as an object. When that subject itself is treated as an object, objectivity itself is missed. Hence, the human subject or self slips through a pure objective analysis.

The phenomenological approach

In a way, the phenomenological approach to the self in experience corrects the above defect and tries to understand man in his phenomenological aspect, as the pure subjectivity involved in every perception. Knowledge presents the world as a system, each element of which receives its meaning from the totality in which it is included. This one meaning is present to me in my own life, the consciousness 'I live'. This 'I live' is expressed in relation to the totality of the universe in the 'I know'. This is a subject-object relation. Subject is identical with consciousness and opposed to the object, yet it is subject only in reference to the object, and the latter is object essentially as something 'known'. Hence, the phenomenon of knowledge manifests a subject-object unity in the bond of knowledge, which is synthetic and creative.

Thus, in consciousness, the human self becomes manifest. The meaning of the universe as well as of my own self appears closely bound up in the experience of my life. My experience is an act, and also a project, comprising all the particular objects in its total meaning. In the context of the act, each particular factor and object appears directed to a goal and meant for an end and, in this sense, manifests the totality of the universal meaning. As the human act comprehends the universe of things, each object becomes a universal, a specification of a universal meaning, a 'tool' for achieving (or rather, revealing) the total meaning of the system and, at the same time, a concretion of one's personal life.

This concretion of the personal being in the vitality of act is especially evident in knowing and willing. Knowledge of anything is also simultaneously self-knowledge. The deeper it goes into the nature of things, the deeper it also penetrates into the nature of the knowing subject. Hence, the centrifugal tendency of knowledge is also centripetal. Already constituted and oriented towards an end, it is at the same time also self-discovering, and therefore personalizing. Similarly, the volitional activity, which is manifested not only in pure desires and decisions, but in sensitive appetites and bodily tendencies as well, on the one hand draws everything, individual things as well as the universe, into its volitional sphere; it is also self-constituting : it manifests the human being as a conscious, free and autonomous self.

Thus, the whole universe of beings manifests itself as a structure and matrix of factors, which at the same time reveals the human self. The factors involved in this structure are in no way static. They extend outwards in a centrifugal force and, at the same time, manifest a centripetal tendency; on the one hand, comprehending all things in a single universal meaning, they also reveal, on the other hand, the human self as the totality and unity of the universal meaning.

But the basic defect of the phenomenological approach is that it fails to bring out the spiritual excellence of man and his transcendence over the whole material universe. What is bound together in a common structure with the universe can never go beyond the universe. Spirituality, immortality and consciousness—all become mere functions of the subject-object structure. For something structured, to go beyond the structure will be to destroy itself. The strength of a chain is in its weakest link; the value of the subject-object structure has to be measured by the individual, changing, limited and concrete object.

From Experience to the Conscious Self

The method of transcendence

In sharp contrast to the phenomenological approach that stops with the structure of consciousness, the Sâmkhyan search for the Ultimate Reality makes use of the method of transcendence. Structure of consciousness helps it to go beyond the structure, and to postulate the existence of the pure spirit, or *Purusha*. The reasons for affirming the existence of the *Purusha* are stated briefly in the seventeenth Kârikâ : 'The spirit exists, since composite objects are other-centred, since it is the reverse of that which has the three attributes and the rest, since there must be control, since there must be someone who enjoys, and since there is activity for release.' A cursory examination of these points will show the main lines of transcendence followed by Indian tradition.

(i) *Structure is Other-Centred* (*samkhâta parârthatvât*) : As Gaudapada says, interpreting this phrase, anything composed of several factors and structured is not a self. Cotton is spun into thread and woven into cloth, not for the sake of the cotton, but only for the sake of the body which it is meant to cover. It has no meaning in itself, but only in reference to something outside itself : in this case, the body. A footstool has no meaning in itself as a wooden structure, but only in reference to the feet for which it is made. Any structure is the putting together of several factors. Each of them is incomplete and inadequate. Neither can all the parts put together produce the unitary meaning. A structure is not merely the sum total of parts, but rather the harmony of factors, a certain unity which cannot be obtained from pure plurality. Structure by itself presents an anomaly : a unity which cannot be explained by the sum total of parts. Unity does not come from multiplicity. That 'something is many' means that none of the individuals has all the perfection indicated by the thing. Multiplicity means distinction—in other words, that one has something, that another has not. Hence, the unity of the structure, the harmony of parts, should be grounded in something beyond the structure. The many involved in a structure point outside the structure for its intelligibility.[6]

---

[6] Vacaspati Misra faces the objection that a structured thing, e.g. a bed-stead, may exist for the sake of another structured thing, the human body, and so on *ad infinitum*. His answer is that, since the reason for postulating something higher than structure is the structured condition, this postulate cannot be satisfied until the unstructured is finally reached; a regress to infinity does not solve the problem (*loc cit.*, pp. 79–81).

Artha, or intelligibility, in the phrase *parârthatvât*, can mean several things : the source from which, the agent by whom, the goal to which, and especially the ground and ideal in which, the totality or the harmony of parts becomes meaningful. Nothing can come out of nothing. Hence, the emergence of structure consisting of several parts presupposes a ground and source of absolute simplicity and unity. Any limited reality is anomalous. Limitation is a negation of reality. The authentic reality, pure and simple, cannot contain its opposite—negation. Therefore, if any reality is found with limitation, it means that it is not the authentic real, but something which merely reflects and manifests the real. It is merely an image of the authentic real to which it essentially points.

Hence, any structure which is only a network of the limited and conditioned is, by its very nature, a veil cast over the authentic real. On the one hand, it hides its authentic character, and, on the other, in as much as it is real, it manifests the Real beyond. A veil is not considered a thing. It is something functional. Its whole meaning is to hide what is within from outside view, and also to indicate that there is something precious within. Similarly, the structural world manifested in our experience is something functional. It has no meaning in itself, no *svârtha*. Its whole meaning is to point to the authentic beyond it. Hence, it is *parârtha*, other-centred.

This other-centredness of structure is particularly evident in the hierarchy of functions and values that any structure implies. No structure exists all by itself, but rather one structure telescopes into other, and higher, structures implying greater unity and higher simplicity. Thus, the table before me is the harmonious totality of its legs, planks and drawers, but the table itself is only one function in the furniture that makes up my room. The room itself is only one of the functions that make up the totality of the house, and the house itself is integrated into the higher totalities of home, country, world and universe. The higher the structure, the more comprehensive of parts it is. Yet, in it, the individuality of the parts becomes less marked and unity more emphasized. This means that any structure is kept in position, not from below by the infrastructure of its parts, but rather from above by a supreme ideal. In the ascending process of structures, the universe itself appears as the manifestation of an all-comprehensive idea.

Anything structured is not supported by itself, but has its meaning outside itself in an Omega point from which it is kept in position. This supreme point of harmony or idea is the ground for the unity of the whole structure, and for that very reason is not part of the structure. It is the norm for judging all that comes within the structure and so is not itself measured. Hence, it is the self, existing in itself and for itself.

(ii) *It is the Reverse of the Evolving World of Experience* : A fascinating point about Sâmkhya-Yoga philosophy is that it looks very anthropomorphic. It wants to explain experience as much as possible in terms of its own dynamism. The Self does not appear as an arbitrary postulate, but rather as the culminating point of a counter-movement implied in experience itself.

There are three irreducible and ultimate functions discernible in our experience : reflectivity, creativity, and limitation or finitude. Thought or capacity to receive the forms of other things in our mind, and to double back on our own actions, is the most dominant note of human experience. Thought breaks the barrier of one's own individuality and brings the subject to the awareness of a great number of possibilities. Hence, it becomes a plan for action, every concept a project to be executed by creativity. Mere conceptual knowledge of things is not satisfying. It is only an image of the thing, which rouses the desire for attaining the thing as fully as it is in itself, and to expand the field of experience to ever-widening fields.

But the limitation of the creative powers of man, the opaqueness of the field of objects, the determinateness and particularity of the avenues of approach, block the outward movement of creativity on all sides. This function of darkness (*tamas*) or finitude, obstructing and individualizing creativity, has at the same time the capacity to reverse the whole movement. It does not and cannot destroy creativity. It only turns the dynamism back on the Self, the source of all intelligibility and creativity. It orients the attention back to the thinking subject.

By its very nature, this reverse process is opposed to the method of experience. If experience is conceptualizing, constructing and individualizing, the reverse reflexion moves away from the concrete and conceptual. In experience, we note a logical synthesis between two concepts which form the subject and predicate of a sentence : a predicative synthesis by which the subject apprehends a particular object, a subjective synthesis in which sense experience and intellectual perception combine to provide a total view of the thing, an objective synthesis between the sensible qualities of the thing and the intelligible essence, and finally a veritative synthesis in which the object is perceived as a truth and a fact independent of and imposing itself on the knowing subject. But in the reverse reflexion, there is a certain decoding of all these complex structures. When the veritative synthesis is recorded, it becomes evident that truth is primarily and formally a characteristic of the knowing and affirming subject, rather than a mere function of the object. The objective synthesis resolves itself into a series of concentric circles of name and form, individuality and specific nature, notes of individuality, principle of individuation, numeric multiplication of a specific nature, all reflexions and refractions of an ultimate and absolute reality which do not add anything to the latter's fullness. The subjective synthesis reveals the same concentric circles around the Self within the thinking subject.

Similarly, knowledge is not merely the construction of a thing as an object, independent of and opposed to the subject, but rather the self-awareness and self-fulfilment expressed in the 'I know' with reference to a particular object. The object is not seen as something totally other. Rather, in knowledge, the subject realizes its own ontological reality as already being in communion with the thing referred to as object. Hence, the predicative synthesis, when decoded, is a deeper insight into the self. For the same reason, knowledge is not a mere logical synthesis, mere conceptualization. Concept is only the presence of the sensed object to the conscious self. To arrive at the Self from it, a process of deconceptualization is called for. All that can be conceived has to be denied, yet this process cannot end in pure negativity. Only what can be conceived can be denied. It should culminate in the pure 'I-hood', the *Purusha*.

Thus, the unavoidable and uneliminable ultimate of all reflexion is the 'I'. The dynamic and functional unity of reflectivity, action and limitation by the weight of the whole complexity, falls back on the pure self as the ultimate ground.

(iii) *The Spiritual Control*: The phenomenon of direction and order in the material realm, and in the universe in general, has always been a cogent reason for postulating a *Nous*, an intelligent controlling principle. Consistent order and effective goal-directedness cannot be explained by chance. When there are only a few factors in operation, certain combinations may occur by chance, but when there is a multitude of factors involved, a consistent and goal-oriented order requires the discernment of the suitable from the unsuitable, choice of some and elimination of many of the possibles; all these call for intelligence, a spiritual directive principle.

But a point emphasized by Indian tradition is that the controlling spiritual principle, *Purusha*, is not itself involved in the movement. Spirit's actions are knowledge and love, intellection and volition. These do not imply by themselves any change or modification, though they may presuppose change in the finite subjects. Hence, they are not actions in the ordinary sense of the term. Spirit's control and direction over the material realm is, therefore, best designated as witnessing. The witness is not a mere spectator, though he is not involved in and affected by the event. He participates in the event by knowledge and consent.

There is, in this, a certain parallelism between the microcosm of the human organism and the macrocosm. Actions within the human organism, as far as they are human, are controlled by the spirit by knowledge and volition. Neither of these actions is material; nor do they exercise any mechanical or physical force on the bodily powers or organs. But the whole complex of actions derives its motive force, reality and meaning from the spirit.

(iv) *The Enjoyer*: As was pointed out in the first reason, the meaning of a structure is not in its parts, nor in the mere totality of parts, but rather in the harmony, unity and finality of the whole. This unity is not realized by the members of the structure from within the structure, but rather, from above the structure. The harmony does not look inwards, where the distinction and particularity of parts stand out. It is directed outwards to a common purpose towards which each of the parts is an instrument. Hence, the meaning of the structure is realized and enjoyed only by one who dominates it. When a room is seen decorated and well furnished and the bed laid out, one does not imagine that it is merely for the sake of the room. The goal and purpose of the whole arrangement is the enjoyment of the one who can realize the meaning of the whole arrangement and profit from it.

Yet the one for whom the structure is constituted does not depend on the structure. If he happens to be actually dependent, it will only show that the enjoyer is limited and imperfect and in some way part of a certain structure himself, and so looks to another beyond. This outward orientation of the structured reality will be eliminated only when One fully independent of all structure is reached. Hence, the Absolute Person is postulated as the ultimate goal and centre of all complexity and composition falling within our conscious experience.

THE INTERNAL UNITY OF EXPERIENCE

The postulate of the Person as the ultimate and authentic reality does not mean that the world of experience is just a mass of un-related entities. Experience, though complex in its components, manifests a certain unity. It is the same 'I' that thinks, acts and feels. None of these three appears in isolation. My thought involves an active encounter with the environment where I meet with a certain resistance to my knowledge and activity. Similarly, every truly human activity is accompanied by the consciousness 'I act', allied with a certain awareness of the object that blocks my out-ward movement. Thus, my experience has a certain cyclic flow, first opening out to the world, which becomes thereby dynamically re-constituted in my experience and, limiting and restricting my activity, turns my attention back to my own depth.

Here the key word is proportion : thought has to be commen-surate with action and the outside reality. Passive acquiescence to material goods will be slavery to their fascination. Action without thought can be dissipating. Thought alone, without action and encounter with the world, will be unrealistic and sterile. Hence, a balance among these three functions of experience are necessary to keep it realistic and fruitful.

The inward movement implied in experience, indicated above, serves to make the proportion and balance productive in insight. Experience leads to thought, thought leads to reflexion, and re-flexion to realization of the ultimate self in its uniqueness. Hence, experience has a consistent structure which does not leave gaps. Everything appearing in experience is explainable in terms of its unique structure. Only for ultimate explanations in terms of reality, existence and personality has it to point beyond itself.

METAPHYSICS OF 'STATE'

From what we have said so far, it has been sufficiently hinted that Hindu tradition does not approach the problem of reality with the pattern of pure phenomenon, nor with that of action. Its pattern of approach is that of concentric levels or states of reality. Once experience or action brings out the nature of a particular state of things, through soundings in that state one can discover what the authentic and ultimate state of reality is, and, on the other hand, also indicate the intermediary as well as the outer levels of the same.

The pattern of approach also determines the fundamental principles of reasoning. Where the state of things is the pattern, the basic principles are not the principles of contradiction, sufficient reason and causality which govern the field of action. These principles have their special relevance where action is the pattern for epistemology and metaphysics. The principle of contradiction says that a thing cannot be itself and its opposite at the same time, otherwise the act of affirmation and apprehension which makes the thing its object will have no meaning; to mean one thing and its opposite is to mean nothing. But this principle does not imply that reality itself is static, and that it has to remain immutably the same in any given time. Similarly, the principle of sufficient reason emphasizes the intelligibility of the thing as the object of perception, and of the act of apprehension. The principle that every contingent should have a cause, the principle of causality, is simply the law of action; no one can give what he has not got.

When the state of reality is taken as the pattern, certain other suppositions form the starting point. The intelligence of the one who tries to understand reality is taken for granted, and inevitably becomes the focal point for all reality as the centre of consciousness. Even the one who doubts, knows; in other words, he knows at least that he doubts. Even he who is under illusion must be a conscious subject; illusion is the clouding of consciousness. This conscious centre or self becomes a sort of common centre for the concentric circles of the various grades of reality presented in experience. Certain norms of evaluation also have to be assumed. These are basically the laws of consciousness.

The changeless and immutable condition is assumed to be the authentic state of reality, while all change and addition is conceived as an accidental modification. This is actually the principle of contradiction applied to the pattern of state : the true condition or essential state of a thing is that which always remains the same in all vicissitudes, while the changing aspects are judged accessory, as owing to the particular conditions of time or place.

Similarly, the condition of the 'I' is taken as the more authentic in preference to the condition of the object or the 'Thou'. For any knowledge and any investigation, the 'I-hood' of the investigator and his capacity to know are the basic suppositions. The existence or reality of any object can be questioned and doubted without prejudice to the inquiry. But if the reality of the conscious self which is the central point of reference is called into question, the very meaning of the inquiry and of knowledge becomes doubtful.

Hence, the region of absolute reality should be located in the core and depth of the conscious self. But, this is not the individual self characterized by the specific nature and concrete limiting adjuncts, but the ultimate ground and centre of its consciousness and I-hood. Therefore, the ultimate and authentic state of reality is the ground and source of all things, the pure and ultimate self, the spirit.

Around the spirit, in no way intrinsically affecting it, there appear several concentric circles of reality in decreasing consciousness and increasing variety of actions, modifications and individual determinations. On the one hand, the whole area of these conditioned levels of existence shows a necessary reference to the self, because they are only 'ek-sistence', a projection, a manifestation, not adding anything to the reality of the spirit. On the other hand, they have a certain independent reality of their own, since they cannot be totally reduced to the spirit. Spirit is immutable; the whole range of the evolving nature shows constant flux, both centrifugal and centripetal, and at the same time a certain organic unity.

The Soul-Body Pattern : This spirit-matter polarity and interrelation should have been suggested by the human organism itself. The word *Atman*, which designates the self in prephilosophic language, is the reflexive pronoun. The body is what it is only through actuation by the spiritual self, the soul.

Hence, the body is, in a sense, a continuation of the soul manifesting its vitality and consciousness. Even the most spiritual ideas and desires of the spiritual self are expressed, manifested and communicated through the gestures and signs of the body, and the bodily expressions in their turn lead to a deeper understanding of the spiritual meaning, and so to a better self-realization.

On the other hand, the bodily organism constitutes a certain unity, with a certain balance between reflexion, action and individuality in every action, expression and aspect. It is, therefore, in a certain sense an object by itself and hides the spiritual reality of the self.

This microcosm of the human being is easily taken as a model for all reality in man's spontaneous quest for an understanding of the macrocosm, the complex world of experience that confronts him.

THE SUPREME SELF AND THE INDIVIDUAL SELVES

Reasons for postulating a spiritual self fall into two categories. Some of them point to an absolute and infinite spirit, others to an individual and finite spirit, but the difference between these two selves is not easily realized in philosophical thought. We find, therefore, two philosophical trends concerning the self.

One postulates an Absolute Spirit as the Unique Self of all, moving and activating every individual thing, a cosmic *Nous*, a universal 'agent intellect', a cosmic *Brahman* who is also *Atman* in relation to individual beings. This Supreme Self is postulated as the ultimate and immutable ground of all reality, the pure and infinite consciousness, the source of all selfhood.

The other trend places the emphasis on the individuality of the self. The very effort to attain liberation from the present state of suffering implies that there is a self to be liberated, a self now bound in the particular conditions of individual existence. Similarly, personal responsibility and freedom of choice, existence of other individual selves made evident by the difference in situations of birth and death, conditions and sorts of different people, all make one's own personal individuality an undeniable fact. This trend, which is represented by the Sâmkhya school, affirms the existence of a good number of individual selves.

However, the difficulty here is that those who concentrate attention on the Absolute and Immutable Self tend to explain away the importance of the individual self as something transitory, a mere negation superimposed on the Real, and, as such, eventually to be eliminated by final realization. Those, on the other hand, who emphasize the individuality and multiplicity of selves easily stop short at the immediate selfhood and do not proceed to the notion of the Supreme Self, which is mistaken for a mere abstract concept, a projection to the infinite of one's idea of selfhood.

A reconciliation between these two trends, a clear distinction between the Absolute Self and the individual selves, is achieved only at a later and more evolved stage of abstract thought. The absolute and all-exclusive nature of the pure spirit does not deny or exclude the uniqueness or individuality of the human self. Similarly, a recognition of the spiritual nature of the individual human spirit does not make the Supreme Self a mere abstraction. Rather, a proper understanding of the individual finite conscious self, gifted with freedom and control over the material realm, facilitates a certain realization of the nature of the self of one's own self. The Divine Self is not known as an object, but rather as the depth and ground of 'I-hood', the fulfilment and goal of my freedom!

The Sâmkhya-Yoga systems are, however, expressly concerned with the dynamics of spirit-matter relationship within the individual. *Sâmkhya Kârikâ* clearly stated that the purpose of the union between *Purusha* and *Prakriti* was their common benefit, like the blind man carrying the lame and the latter showing the way; they have a common goal to attain.[7] Matter reaches its full evolution, and spirit attains liberation. According to Vacaspati Misra, this liberation is isolation of the spirit through the discrimination of its otherness from the *gunas* of *Prakriti*.[8] Gaudapada, on the other hand, emphasizes the reaching of a common destination;[9] *Prakriti*, the blind, attains a point of undisturbed quiet in the balance of *gunas*; and *Purusha* attains unimpeded vision of its own spiritual reality. The later Sâmkhya school, represented by the *Sâmkhya Sûtras*, places the accent on the self-realization of *Purusha*: by throwing light on the inner organ, it is led back to the source of light within itself; the inner organ presents an image of the spirit which leads to self-realization.

On the whole, a philosophy constructed in terms of the dynamics of the spirit is centred on the personality of the spiritual being. This individual personality has a certain inner openness to the Absolute Spirit. On the other hand, it also implies a close relationship with the body structure. This relationship is one of distinction and opposition, and also of complementarity. This philosophy, dealing as it does with the deepest concerns of man, especially with the meaning of the ultimate goal of human life, is religion, at least in the general sense of the term.

[7] *Sâm K, Kârikâ* 21.
[8] *The Tattva Kaumudi*, p. 90.
[9] *Gaudapada Bhâshya*, pp. 65-6.

CHAPTER X
INTUITION, BASIS OF VEDANTIC METAPHYSICS

The Vedantic tradition goes beyond the logical and psychological levels of experience and tries to attain immediate realization of absolute reality which is pure, immutable and infinite consciousness. The only important problem here is how one who is bound in bodily existence can get beyond the limitations of experience. Here, Vedânta starts from man's intense desire to be liberated from this world of ignorance and suffering and to attain the immutable absolute reality. It proceeds by taking the world of experience as something originating, and therefore limited. This world is, accordingly, a symbol of the beyond. Here, the statements of ancient sages put down in scripture provide guidelines for man's spiritual pilgrimage beyond this world. Basing itself on these, Vedânta tries to formulate an integral vision of the Ultimate Reality in which man's selfhood is grounded.

The standard text-book of the Vedânta school is the *Vedânta Sûtras*, ascribed to the sage Badarâyana. The school produced a number of eminent thinkers and religious leaders like Sankara, Ramanuja, Vallabha, Nimbarka, and others. It would be presumptuous to attempt here a complete treatment of the whole Vedânta school, detailing the contributions of different authors. I shall therefore merely present here what appears to me to be the most basic contribution of the school, namely its idea of intuition, which is a break-through in our worldly experience to get a glimpse of the ultimate reality. In this, I shall restrict myself to the doctrine of Sri Sankaracharya, the undisputed leader of the school.

According to Sankara, *anubhava,* or intuition, is the goal of investigation into the nature of ultimate reality, for only in matters depending on one's will and pleasure are different opinions possible; only in these can personal judgment and taste be taken as the criterion. For things which actually exist, different opinions cannot all be ultimately valid. For example, concerning a post, one is not free to state that it is a man or something other than a post; it has to be recognized as a post, and, in this, immediate experience is the criterion. Post is its own ultimate criterion, and it is known by direct contact. Reality is its own criterion and has to be judged by its own light. Any alien light will only distort it. Hence, intuition is the only adequate means for attaining reality.

DIFFERENT MEANINGS OF INTUITION

Intuition itself has been differently understood in different systems, according to different angles of approach. Knowledge itself can be taken as the presence of the intelligible object in the intelligent subject, or as the conscious activity by which the subject grasps the object, or as the moment of consciousness in which the subject and object are united in the same spiritual actuality.

In the objectivist meaning, intuition is the presence of the intelligible in the intelligent without any mediating factor—whether it be the spiritualized concept with regard to material things, or the alien species in which things above the particular condition of the knower are understood. Thus, the beatific vision of God by the created intellect constitutes an intuition because the Divine Intelligible directly terminates the created intellect.

But when the accent in knowledge is placed on the act of knowing, intuition may, in general, be taken as a direct approach to what is presented to the mind without the aid of intermediary steps which in some manner imply it. This direct approach may be taken in a strict or broad sense. The perception of beauty in a bouquet of flowers is said to be an intuition, since beauty is not merely the flowers heaped together, but their proper order and arrangement which is above and beyond experience through the senses. Even perception of the idea of a flower in the complexity of the experience of colour, touch, and smell can be considered an intuition, since these sensations do not constitute but only point to the intelligible essence. But those who emphasize the synthetic character of even our intellectual perceptions and the great many judgments implied in them will not call them intuitions. Intuition is taken in this broad sense when it is applied to the perception of values and goodness. In these, the final act of knowledge is not merely the adding up of all the preceding acts, but there is a new act of an encounter between an integrated subject and an integrated object, though the final encounter has been prepared by the series of acts that went before it.

Intuition of Reality : This direct encounter is clearly present in the perception of reality as such. It is not merely the addition of a new idea to the mental deposit of impressions, but the recognition of something as existent. When I proceed from the idea of the table to the statement 'the table is', I may not get any better knowledge of what a table is, but I realize that the table is a fact integral to the totality of the actual world, and my affirmation of it is a truth. This is a direct encounter with reality.

This encounter with reality *qua* reality can be interpreted in different ways, and different avenues of approach are open to the investigator. An objectivist approach will analyze the very meaning of objectivity : reality is the object of thought and knowledge. Even to have an idea is to have the idea of 'some thing'—something opposed (*ob-jectum*) to the mind, in front of the mind. This is particularly true in the idea of being, which refers something to existence as actually existing, or as being possible to exist, or as incompatible with existence. Every one of our judgments takes out some idea of essence from the area of mere impressions and concepts, and refers it to the field of existence, actual or possible— the world of reality.

In this reference to existence, a certain intuition is involved. Whether one views the object purely in its objectivity—in its aspect of being opposed to the mind—or in its inner meaning as something intelligible in itself, or in the perfection of existence in contrast to non-existence, these aspects can in no way be reduced to mere sense experience. The intellectual apprehension of these aspects of the object goes beyond the field of the senses.

When a certain point is not deduced from or explained in terms of some other thing in which it is implied, but is merely seen or perceived in itself, this can also be considered an intuition. Thus, even when abstracting from a preconceived objectivity, the understanding of phenomenological structure demands a direct perception or intuition. Structure is not merely a collective picture of sense-data. It is complex and hierarchical. From the lowest level of the unity of the sense-data in a single perceived object, there is a scale proceeding upwards through the four levels of Plato's divided line, ending in absolute unity. The One is the ultimate value of reality, and goodness is its dynamic counterpart which shows its diffusion down the scale.

Metaphysical systems have even endeavoured to go beyond this scale. In India tradition, the Sâmkhya school tries to go beyond this structural objectivism with the basic argument: *samghâta parârthavât*—all structure is for the sake of another. Structure is not a mere togetherness or co-existence of factors, but a purposeful arrangement pointing beyond itself towards something else. Hence, Sâmkhya metaphysics postulates that the ultimate condition of reality is either a dynamic balance of irreducible functions in a single material and maternal principle, or/and the pure motionless unity of consciousness. This means the perception in things of two ultimate principles: *Prakriti*, the self-evolving maternal principle of all material things, and *Purusha*, the pure spirit, which is unaffected by the evolutions of the material world. These principles cannot be said to be implied in ordinary experience. Perception of these principles beyond structures is still a different kind of intuition from the one which simply detects the harmony of parts.

The method of Sankara's intuition

Sankara and the Vedânta school in general follow another method of approach to attain an intuition of reality. Instead of unifying and building up the world of multiplicity into a harmony of values, they proceed by denying the validity of the multiplicity: in the complexity of our experience, the path to reality is one of negation, rather than one of affirmation. However, this negation does not end in a negative conception, but in a stronger affirmation and a more positive grasp of reality. To put it another way, the ground for this denial is the ultimate and absolute unity of all reality taken for granted.

The Negative Approach in Hindu Tradition: This cautious and negative approach to the world of experience neither indicates a pessimistic outlook on the world, nor flows from a conviction of the ineffability of the Ultimate. It is a characteristic note of Indian philosophical thought, discernible even in the earliest literature. The basic human moral outlook is stated in two negative terms: *a-himsa* and *a-bhaya*, which are, however, very positive in meaning.[1] *Ahimsa* literally means non-killing or non-violence, but in-

---

[1] Cf. *Chând Up*, III, 17, 4; *Mahabharata*, 13, 141, 25; *Ahimsaparano dharma, Manu Smriti*, 12, 83; *Mahabharata*, 1, 11, 13.

cludes the positive ideas of compassion, humanity, kindness, fellow feeling; *abhaya* is fearlessness, which includes not only freedom from fear, but also harmony, balance and perfect agreement between body and soul. According to the *Yoga Sûtras* of Patanjali, *ahimsa* implies abstinence from malice towards all creatures, truthfulness, honesty, continence, etc.[2]

Similarly, the ideal condition of life and eternal vitality is designated by *a-mrita*, freedom from death.[3] Health and well-being are expressed by *a-klesa* = absence of fatigue[4] and *a-roga* = absence of sickness.[5] Right conduct is expressed in negative terms like *a-droha*, freedom from malice and also benevolence, and *a-krodha*, suppression of anger and also placidity and serenity. This way of expressing positive ideas in negative terms is not entirely lacking in Western thought. We have examples like secure (*sine cura* = without anxiety) which means confident, and sedulous (*sine dolo* = without deceit) which means diligent and persevering. But this is not a common or characteristic mode of expression, as it is in Indian tradition.

This negative approach is more appropriate in describing the Supreme Reality, about which it is easier to say what it is not than to give any proper definition of it. The *Rig Veda* speaks of gods Agni and Indra as *anûna*, without defect, implying that they are complete and perfect.[6] The Upanishads call God *akshara*, imperishable,[7] *adrisya*, unperceivable, *agrâhya*, ungraspable, *agotra*, without family, *avarna*, without caste,[8] *ajam*, the unborn,[9] *akâyam*, bodiless, *avarnam*, invulnerable, *asnâviram*, devoid of sinews.[10]

This negative approach may have been inspired in the beginning by a ritual preoccupation with avoiding all inaccuracy in words. A pessimistic outlook on the world of change and suffering from which one longed to be freed may also have been in the background. However, in later philosophical development, this way of negation was the first step in a realistic evaluation of experience.

---

[2] *Yog S*, II, 30. Cf. P. V. Kane, *History of Dharmasastra*, II, 1 (1941), p. 10.
[3] *Brih Up*, I, 3, 28.
[4] *Manu Smriti*, IV, 3.
[5] *Ibid.*, VII, 226.
[6] *RV*, I, 146, 1; II, 10, 6; VI, 17, 4; *AV*, XII, i, 11.
[7] *Mûnd Up*, I, i, 4; *Kath Up*, I, iii, 2.
[8] *Mûnd Up*, I, i, 6.
[9] *Brih Up*, IV, iv, 22.
[10] *Isa Up*, 8.

Sankara was one of the principal representatives of this method
and an important exponent of it. This metaphysical procedure
towards the intuition of reality, clearly set forth in his introduction
to the *Vedânta Sûtra Bhâshya*, the commentary on the *Sûtras* of
Badarâyana, can be summarized in the following steps :—

(1) *The Anomaly of Experience* : Experience shows an irreducible opposition, and at the same time an inextricable confusion,
between the areas of the concepts of I and Thou, subject and
object. The subject, the area of the concept of I-hood, is the
knower, and the object, the area of the Thou, is the known. They
are opposed to each other and are irreconcilable as light and
darkness, and their properties are too opposed to each other. But,
in the process of knowledge, the area of the objective Thou comes
to be superimposed on the I. Anything is known only to the extent
that it becomes involved in and is presented through the conscious
experience of the knower. It is a diffusion of the subjectivity of
the knower as seen in statements like 'That am I', 'Thine is mine'.
One's personal interpretation of a thing is often taken for the reality
itself. In reverse, the pure conscious and spiritual subject assumes
the material conditions such as 'I suffer', 'I desire', and so on. All
the means of right knowledge, including sense experience, rational
inference made from such experience, tradition, and even revelation, are inextricably tied up with this subject-object confusion.
Hence, any attempt to discover a harmony in order to get beyond
this confusion will only go deeper into it, since the only way open
is the same duality.

(2) *Structure of Erroneous Perception* : The basic structure of
an erroneous perception shows that the attempt to get to absolute
reality by synthesizing and structuring our experience is futile, for
structure itself is the basic factor in any erroneous perception.
Error is not a mere negation. It is a proposition like any other
statement. A good many theories have been proposed to explain
the nature of error. The basic fact is that the root of all error is
in the confusion of empirical data presented to consciousness. When
data, once experienced and retained in memory, are confused with
other data, or attributed to wrong subjects, or formulated in conscious statements, there is error. This may be the attribution of the
properties of one subject to another, or details of one situation to
another, or even the projection of a mental form on a non-existent
subject. In any case, there is the 'apparent presentation of the

attributes of one thing in another thing'—namely, confusion in consciousness of two distinct fields. Sankara argues that this confusion is the basic condition of empirical and synthetic knowledge : a synthesis of impressions and of conceptions is impossible without subjectifying the object and objectifying the subject, and thus distorting both.

(3) *Metaphysical 'Inscendence' through Intuition* : The way out of this mental quagmire is intuition of the self. Different terms are used to indicate this intuition : *âtmasâkshâtkâra*=direct perception of oneself, *aparokshajnâna* = not-indirect-knowledge, and *âtmabodha* = self-realization. Sankara introduces the discussion of this point with an objection : if the self is a non-object and totally unconnected with the area of the Thou, how can it be known at all? The answer is that the self is not absolutely a non-object; it is the object of the sense of 'I'. Besides, it is perceived in a 'non-indirect' (*a-paroksha*) fashion. The self is present in every perception and affirmation. But it is not *pratyaksha*, the direct object of perception. Nor is it *paroksha*, the indirect object, which is beyond the object and yet is known in and through the object, by an analysis of the direct object. It is the *a-paroksha*, non-indirect term of knowledge, attained through an operation which is in the opposite order to that of perception. This is a de-structuralization of the act of knowledge. Knowledge is a building up, a synthesis. Perception of the self is denying the structure to perceive the builder behind it. Every conception can be denied, but the one who denies cannot be denied, and the ground of denial itself cannot be denied. Descartes proceeded from the *cogito* to the *sum*, thereby exteriorizing consciousness in the 'ek-sistence'. Sankara proceeds in the opposite direction, interiorizing consciousness in order to see its simplest and irreducible form after removing every suprastructure. Perhaps this procedure merits the term 'intuition' (*intus-ire*) : the conscious self goes deeper into itself by denying all that can be conceived and constructed.

The inward movement is not artificial, nor arbitrarily postulated. The very anomaly of the I-Thou opposition indicates a spontaneous movement inwards to the depths of the self to resolve the anomaly. Knowledge is not an action in the ordinary sense of the term. It is not a movement or a change. Its characteristic note is actuality. Nor is it an outward movement to dissipate oneself in the exteriority of the senses and of the objects, but rather an attempt to regain one's own authentic centre by raising the material world surrounding and hiding the self to the level of its own spiritual luminosity. The Sâmkhya philosophers clearly understood this centripetal direction of knowledge when they stated that all evolution in the material world has for its natural goal the self-consciousness of *Purusha*; the spirit is trying to reach its own consciousness in, through and with the material surrounding. Only in the conscious self can other things find their meaning and intelligibility. Other knowing subjects especially can be properly reached only in and through the interiority of the self. The imperfection of consciousness, the I-Thou duality, and, according to Sankara, even the plurality of conscious subjects, all show that the knowing subject is not in its authentic condition of consciousness.

The negative categories of Hindu thought discussed earlier—for instance, *a-himsa*, *a-bhaya*, etc.—imply a double negation which strongly emphasizes this inward movement. *Ahimsa* is the negation of *himsa*, or violence, which itself is a baneful involvement in the external realm. The denial of violence therefore signifies liberation from this involvement, a strong affirmation of one's being centred in oneself, being thereby benevolently disposed towards others. Similarly, *bhaya* is the condition of being subjected to the threat of and danger from the outside world, and its denial means confidence in one's own depth and a calm attitude towards others. As Sankara repeatedly explains, the root of fear is in finding the world of the Thou as a rival to the I. When the ek-sistence of the world can be looked upon as an extrapolation of and reflexion from the ultimate centre of consciousness, and when other selves can be met within the Supreme Self, all fear is removed.

(4) *Brahmajijnâsâ*: The dynamic nature of this intuition is expressed in the first *Sûtra* of Badarâyana: 'Then, therefore, the desire to know Brahman.' This *jijnâsâ*, intense desire to know, is the first moment of the intuition. It is not a mere curiosity to find out the unity, meaning and purpose of the world of multiplicity. Unity within the self is taken for granted. That unity cannot be built up by an outward movement. The *jijnâsâ* in question is the quest for one's own identity. It is not particularly concerned with the existence or non-existence of finite things. One who is attached to finite things obstructs his own view of the infinite, but the way out is not the denial of the finite. As Nagarjuna stated, centuries earlier than Sankara, one who is preoccupied with denying the

finite world is involved in the same entanglement as the one who is affirming it. Search for the ultimate, which is the basic dynamism of *jijñâsâ*, gains in intensity when the external entanglement of complexity is subdued by *tapas*, austerity, which literally means concentration of energies in oneself. When the dissipated energies are gathered up, the vagaries of passion eliminated, and the spirit established in the quiet of self-possession, the spontaneous movement of consciousness seeks its own fullness. Philosophy does not start in wonder, but in suffering. Suffering which arises out of the complexity of existence is at the same time a *katharsis*, a purification, and also a *katalysis*, a loosening, which generates a certain *ana-lysis*, a resolution of the complexity itself. All three elements are included in the comprehensive word *mumuksha*, an intense desire for liberation from the complexity of worldly attachment. *Môksha* is, therefore, the counterpoint of *jijñâsâ*.

Môksha has been the central ideal for Hindu tradition, but it is not liberation in a negative sense, an escape from a prison into a world of ideas. It is a positive notion which means the integration of all the complexity of finite being in the unifying centre of consciousness. It is a descent into one's ultimate depth in silence. Hence, both *jijñâsâ* and *môksha* are united in *anubhava*; they are only two moments of the 'intu-ition' of absolute consciousness as one's real and ultimate centre.

(5) *Janmâdyasya Yatah—Meaning of the Finite World*: The second *Sûtra* of Badarâyana, 'That from which the origin and the rest', marks a second moment in the intuition, by which the world of multiplicity is shown in its positive meaning. Sankara summarizes the meaning of the world in the term *mâyâ*. *Mâyâ* does not mean 'illusion' for Sankara, though that meaning came to be overemphasized in later *Advaita Vedânta*. In the *Rig Veda*, the word *mâyâ* is used about a hundred times, and it means wisdom, judgment, knowledge, power and energy. Now, these are indifferent in themselves and may be used for good or for evil. For the gods, it is the beneficient power of creativity. All the cosmic phenomena are said to be the result of the divine *mâyâ*. The Maruts bring rain by *mâyâ*.[11] The sun appears in the skies by the *mâyâ* of Mitra and Varuna.[12] Thus, *mâyâ* came to designate the marvels of nature, and

[11] *RV*, I, 88, 1.
[12] *RV*, III, 61, 7.

the divine capacity to attain the marvellous.[13] The gods are called *mâyinâh*, gifted with power.[14] They can produce something new and control the events of men.[15]

But cleverness and power can also be abused. Thus, malicious men use *mâyâ* to fly like birds in order to accomplish their evil purposes.[16] Hence, it is also allied with deceit, delusion, and sometimes taken for the power to produce deceptive forms. Indra obtains his divine position by all kinds of deceits and his capacity for assuming various illusory forms.[17]

Hence, the statement that the world is *mâyâ* has several shades of meaning. It means that the world has no absolute reality, but is the product of the will and pleasure of the Supreme Lord. It states that the existence of the world is not eternal, but transitory, and therefore delusory. It implies that the world is a mystery which cannot be explained in itself.

But the most comprehensive meaning of *mâyâ* is the *janmâd-yasya yatah* : the world is a symbol, a signboard which points away from itself to the source of its origin, subsistence and the final fulfilment. To realize the meaning of the world, one has to look away from it. As Nagarjuna says, one who keeps his eyes fixed on the finger pointing to the moon will never see the moon. He has to move his gaze away from the finger to what it points at.

This designative direction of the world of experience is expressed in the statement of the *Taittirîya Upanishad, 'satyam jnânam anantam Brahman'. Brahman* is immutable and infinite consciousness. The change and instability of the world are anomalies that show that the world is just a shadow of the immutable ultimate reality. Its unintelligibility and materiality are just a veil cast over the pure consciousness of the Supreme; all multiplicity and limitation indicate that they are a refraction of the all-comprehensive fullness.

But, this shadow and reflexion will never give an adequate idea of what the Ultimate Reality is. They only point in the direction of the Ultimate, which can be known only through intuition or immediate realization.

[13] *RV*, V, 63, 4; IX, 83, 3.
[14] *RV*, III, 20, 3.
[15] *RV*, IV, 30, 21; I, 6; X, 53, 9.
[16] *RV*, III, 30, 16.
[17] *RV*, II, 12; III, 53.

This brings out another meaning of intuition. It is not an objective vision of God. A god who can be looked at from the outside is no God. He who says, 'God is', does not know God. God is not an 'it', a thing among other things, nor a 'he', a person among other persons, nor even a 'thou', since no person can face him on a level of equality. God can be known only through *anubhava*, a becoming-one-with-him. Hence, God is both the principle and term of an experience of God. *Brahmaved Brahmaiva bhavati*, he who knows God becomes even God. One can know God only if God reveals himself to him, and so becomes the immediate principle of his activity. The meaning of the world in relation to absolute reality is that of *māyā*, a manifestation of the mysterious power of the Supreme, a reflexion and a symbol pointing towards the Real, a veil that hides the Ultimate.

The metaphysics of intuition

A metaphysics based on such an 'intuition', the *anubhava* of the Ultimate Reality, will differ from the one based on the objective understanding of the world of experience.

Here, being is not the basic and all-embracing concept. Being takes the world of reality as the object of thought and knowledge, that which is opposed to the mind, independent of the mind, and existing in its own right. Intuition bases itself in consciousness, which in reality is centred in itself and, as it were, comprehending its own deepest centre. In relation to it, all being is ek-sistence, an extrapolation.

In such a metaphysics, one does not strive to establish a unity as the ultimate goal of thought. Unity is taken for granted. But it is not the numerical unity of discrete quantity as opposed to a plurality of the same sort, nor a transcendental unity which comprehends the many in a single ideal of cause outside of which and opposed to which there is nothing. Neither is it a unity of harmony by which the many are kept together in a structure more than and higher than the sum total of parts. The unity which Sankara's intuition envisages is the concentration of all reality in a single centre, which does not exclude the possibility of many, not however opposed to it or adding to it, but merely reflecting it. Hence, it cannot be called one or many. The only possible characterization of reality is *a-dvaita*, non-dual.

PHILOSOPHY AND RELIGION

These different philosophical approaches to the basic problems of life and reality present a unique concept of religion. It is not the sum total of concepts, principles, and duties in reference to a definite being designated as 'God'. The Hindu concern is with concrete human life, and Hindu religion is the acknowledgement of the non-finality of the individual human self. The individual conscious self finds itself in the bondage of suffering, limited and restricted by its finiteness.

This is an implicit acknowledgement of an infinite authentic self not affected by ignorance or limitations. This presents a pure concept of God, unaffected by the anthropomorphic qualities with which ordinary theism dresses up its God. Hence, when these so-called atheistic classical schools passed on to a theistic phase in their later development, their idea of God fell far short of the Absolute. For example, the Isvara postulated by the later Nyâya-Vaiseshika philosophers like Sri Udayanacharya, is a mere potter-god who was called in merely to be a guide for the blind force of *adrishta* which grouped together the atoms in various combinations. The Isvara of Patanjali Yoga was merely a liberated individual *Purusha*, who acted, at best, as an elder brother for the individuals seeking liberation.

On the other hand, these different Hindu religious systems did not constitute complete or exclusive religions. They were mostly schools of thought which provided life orientations. The followers of these schools belonged simultaneously to several of the six main religious groups of popular Hinduism, known as *shanmatas*, and practised the cult of a personal deity like Vishnu, Siva, Sakti, Ganapati, Kumara and Surya. Thus, Sri Sankaracharya, who may be considered the most abstract religious metaphysician of India, has also given us some of the most moving devotional literature of Hindu tradition.

The reason for this most paradoxical combination between abstract philosophy and intensely devotional religion may be the practical bent of the Hindu mind. As Jacques Masin remarks, 'the Hindu revolts against ready-made ideas because he is eminently practical and anti-intellectualist'. For him, an idea is not good unless it can be realized in life. Hence, 'Indian schools are not systems, but different ways of corresponding to the state of spiritual progress of each one, and which guide all to the Absolute'.[18] The life and energy of Hindu religion come from this enduring tension between the constant quest of the Absolute and the intensely devotional cult on the popular level, organized according to the needs of the social structure.

[18] *Mélange sur l'Inde,* Vol. I, Special number (June-July, 1941), of *Cahier du Sud,* series *Le trois Lotus,* pp. 21-2.

CHAPTER XI

ISLAM AND THE RELIGIOUS CULTURE
OF INDIA

The evolution of Indian religious culture, as we have it today, is unintelligible without taking into account the Hindu-Muslim encounter which is now over a millennium old. One is consciously influenced by what one appreciates and loves in others, and unconsciously, but more deeply, by what one envies, hates, and fights against in one's adversaries. This is also quite true about Indian religious tradition. Hinduism to a great extent owes what it is today to what Islam was. Islam, too, in spite of all its open protestations to the contrary, was deeply influenced by the stance of Hinduism, and had a unique history of its own on the Indian sub-continent, distinct from the rest of the Muslim world.

MOHAMMED AND ISLAM

Today, Muslims resent the title of Mohammedans, since this might imply that they worshipped Mohammed, but there was a time when they prided themselves on the name *al-umma al-Muhammadiya*. 'There is but one God and Mohammed is his prophet' is a summary of Muslim faith; in this, the prophethood of Mohammed may be considered the more specific and distinguishing note of Islam, since there are other religions which hold monotheism as fervently as Islam. 'Islam' means one 'submitting' oneself to God. 'Muslim' is an adjective from the same root, and 'Musalman' is its Persian form. Historically, the personality, vision and moral character of Mohammed were the central factors in the evolution of Islam as a religion.

Mohammed was born in A.D. 570 into a leading family of Mecca, a wealthy commercial city of Arabia. The familiar evils of a rich business community gave Mohammed the divine call to preach the judgment of God against the wickedness of his society, and to call his

104

countrymen to repentance. Rejection and opposition added fuel to his prophetic zeal and eventually led him to the foundation of the Islamic religion. When he was rejected by the Meccans, he made use of a timely invitation from the warring factions of Medina, a neighbouring city, to be their mediator and spiritual adviser. At Medina, he was able to transform his words into action, and A.D. 622, the year of his departure (*Hijra*) for Medina, became the beginning of the Muslim era. After seven years of struggle, the Meccans, too, willingly followed him. He used diplomacy, and less often military action as well, but only as instruments for exerting religious and moral influence on the rough and undisciplined tribesmen. His whole endeavour was to instruct, organize and train them as a closely knit spiritual community.

Situated at the meeting point of the three powerful kingdoms of the Byzantines, Persians and Ethiopians, the new community became the symbol and spearhead of Arab feeling which struggled for survival and liberation. The humanity of Mohammed was the unifying and energizing factor. As a man, he knew how to temper strict legislation with lenient enforcement. Though he bowed to Arab tradition by sanctioning polygamy and the superior rights of the father and of the husband, by his reforms he also raised the status of women. Before he died, in 632, he was able to see the Muslim community well established, and quickly pushing its territorial boundaries in all directions.

The Koran

The *Koran* or *Quran*, the sacred book of the Muslims, contains the formal discourses and utterances of Mohammed, which are accepted as being directly inspired. It is divided into one hundred and fourteen *Sûras*, or chapters. As may be expected in a community in close contact with the Christian and Jewish communities, its material bears close similarities to their two traditions. It takes strict monotheism for granted—*Lâ ilâha illa'llah* : there is no God but Allah. It agrees with the Jewish tradition in appealing to Abraham as the great common ancestor, and Moses as a prophet. The doctrine which affected Mohammed very deeply was that of the Last Judgment, certainly derived not from Arabic sources, but from the writings of the Syriac Christian fathers and monks. Fear of God is the basic virtue inculcated in the *Koran*, but the mercy of God is also emphasized. Forgiveness is not attained by human merit, but only by the grace of God. To obtain this grace, man has to practise self-control and serve God constantly and faithfully through good works, especially prayer and alms-giving. Against the background of social and spiritual anarchy that prevailed in Arabia, Mohammed had to demand unquestioning obedience and compulsory performance of social and religious duties.

The spread of Islam

Islam spread phenomenally quickly and its influence on the social structure was revolutionary. In 662, the capital of the Muslim community was shifted to Damascus under the Umayyad Caliphs. Within two centuries, the kingdoms of Persia, Mesopotamia, Syria and Egypt came under its domination, and still it continued to push itself into Samarkand, North Africa, and Spain. In 749, the Abbasid dynasty took over the Caliphate and established it at Baghdad. When the Islamic civilization had reached its climax in the 10th and 11th centuries, it had impressed its special character in all areas of human life. Industry, commerce, architecture and the minor arts flourished in the vast expanse of the Muslim world, but the Arabic language, which remained the one language for Muslim literature for over four centuries, was a great handicap in the spread of the civilization itself. Suspicion about the hellenizing influence of philosophy put a ban on rational thought, and the Muslim savants had to devote most of their energy to the study of Sacred Law.

Here, the supreme law was the *Koran*. In the second place came the *sanna*, or the traditions tracing their origin to Mohammed. These traditions constitute a vast literature, known as *Hadith*. The Muslim lawyers had to give the right interpretation of this Sacred Law. In this work they went beyond Roman Law, and, with the emphasis on the religious bases and theocratic sanctions, instated the Sacred Law as the spiritual regulator of the Islamic community. With the ascendancy of the Turkish tribesmen who dominated Persia, the Islamic civilization declined, yet Islam was able to impose its religion, law and tradition on these barbarians.

Even today, Islam is a living faith. It is the religion of over 400 million people in the world. What enabled Islamic religion to survive the Muslim civilization was the clear distinction between religion and state. The Caliphs embodied the supremacy of the Faith and of the Sacred Law. However, they never succeeded in functioning as an orthodox central authority in religion; the learned Ulamas or interpreters of the Law never fully submitted to an institutional authority. The Caliphs were political heads. In that respect, too, together with the Turkish Sultans in Persia, and the Ottoman Empire in Asia and North Africa, their political influence was practically reduced to a minimum from the close of the tenth century. The Muslim rulers, however, recognized and enforced the Islamic Law and imposed a tax, or *jisya*, on non-Muslims.

Islam in India

Islam's first contacts with India were through the Arab traders who, every year, called at the ports of the west coast of India. When they had been converted to Islam, these Arabs did not fail to communicate their newly found faith to their Indian customers and patrons. Already in the earlier part of the eighth century A.D., a small Muslim community came into existence on the Malabar coast. Legend has it that the great Cheraman Perumal, then king of the whole Malabar coast, embraced Islam and, after dividing his kingdom among his governors, went on a pilgrimage to Mecca. The coronation ceremonies of the king of Tranvancore contained certain allusions to this great Mecca-going ancestor. At the court of the Zamurin of Calicut, too, the Muslims gained considerable influence. Though the Muslim invaders had tried to conquer portions of India by the middle of the 8th century during the reign of Caliph Al-Mansur, they were able to get only a precarious foothold in a portion of Sindh. The Muslim conquest of India only came several centuries later.

Sûfi influence

Muslim conquerors, Arabs, Turks and Munghols, were the official arms of Islam entrusted with the task of spreading the religion of Islam and enforcing the Sacred Law. However, a more broadly-based and efficient missionary organ was the Sûfi movement. When the Ummayids had fallen, and the Abasids had become inefficient with the ascendancy of nomadic elements, Sûfi mysticism was the fount of self-renewal in the Muslim community. The name 'Sufi' was originally derived from *sûf*, undyed wool, from the coarse wool garments which these Muslim ascetics wore in imitation of the Nestorian monks of the Middle East. There were later attempts to discover other derivations that would suggest a deeper meaning: some trace it to the word *sâfa*, purity : 'The Sûfi is he whose heart is sincere towards God.' Others take it to mean rank (*sâff*) and imply that the Sûfis hold the first rank before God.[1] Attempts to connect the sûfi term to Greek *sophia* and *sophos* are simply fanciful.[2] Nevertheless, these in a certain sense represented the Sûfi ideal. As formulated by Zakariah Ansari, 'Sûfism teaches how to purify one's self, improve one's morals, and build up one's inner and outer life in order to attain perpetual bliss. Its subject-matter is the purification of the soul and its end or aim is the attainment of eternal felicity and blessedness'.[3]

Naturally, this personal mysticism was always frowned upon and held in suspicion by the officialdom of Islam. Sûfis, on the other hand, have endeavoured to trace their movement to Mohammed himself through the Haddiths or traditions,[4] and to show that their teaching is essentially Koranic. They emphasize the virtues specially inculcated in the *Koran* : purity of heart, obedience to the law, and denial of the pleasures of the world. A Sûfi is severed from the world and connected with God alone. 'At rest in body, contented in mind, broad-chested, his face beaming with the light of God, with an enlightened heart and oblivious of all things due to his nearness with God,' he seeks God alone.[5] The Sûfis identify themselves with the Muqarrabun, those nearest to God, mentioned in the *Koran*,[6] as distinct from the Companions of the Right Hand, the believers, and the Companions of the Left Hand, namely, those who reject faith.

The Sûfi movement soon integrated to itself mystic elements from Neo-Platonism as well as from the Zoroastrian tradition. Among these elements, experience of God in the interior of the heart, and emphasis on the unreality of the world, were important.

The opportunity for the Sûfis to carry out their missionary work on a large scale in India came with the annual expeditions of Muhammood of Gazni into the Indus Valley. He did not found

---

[1] Cf. Mir Valiuddin, *The Quranic Sufism* (Delhi: Motilal Banarsidass, 1959), pp. 1–2.

[2] H. A. R. Gibb, *Mohammedanism, An Historical Survey* (New York: Oxford University Press, 1962), p. 132.

[3] Mir Valiuddin, *op. cit.*, p. 3.

[4] *Ibid.*, p. 4.

[5] *Ibid.*, p. 7.

[6] *Quran Sura*, LVI.

any Indian Empire, nor establish permanent control, except over a small part of the Punjab, yet his victorious marches against the 'infidels' gave great prestige to the Muslim community of India. Conversion or death were the alternatives proposed by Muhammood to the vanquished Hindus. This virulent proselytism swelled the ranks of the Muslim community. Zealous Sûfis made use of the opportunity to carry out their missionary effort deep into the Indo-Gangetic plain. Shaikh Isma'il of Lahore was the first of these Sûfi missionaries. He was followed by Shaikh Ali bin Usman al-Hujairi, and a good many others. Some of these were very holy men and are even today venerated as saints by both Muslims and Hindus. Besides the individual Sûfis, Sûfi orders or religious organizations also found their place in India. The two important Sûfi orders were the Chistis, the disciples of Khvaja Mu'in-ud-din, and the Suhrâwardis, whose founder and leader was Bahâ-ud-din Zakariyâ, who died in 1263.

Various sects of Islam also found representation in the Indian Muslim community. Not long after the death of the prophet Mohammed, Islam had split into two major groups, the orthodox Sunnis and the revolutionary Shi'as. The latter venerated, as a martyr, Ali, the cousin and son-in-law of the Prophet. Though he became Caliph after Mohammed's death, the majority resisted him, and he was murdered by the Umayyads, who led the Sunni group. The Shi'as also hold the doctrine of *Imâms*, sinless and infallible beings, who are supposed to have possessed a secret knowledge communicated by God to Mohammed, and from him to Ali and his descendants. Shi'as, considered a heretical sect by the Arab Muslims, gained influence and power among the non-Arab converts to Islam. These later split up into a number of sub-sects like the 'twelvers' who acknowledged twelve Imâms, the 'Seveners' or Isma'ilis, so called because of a dispute concerning the seventh Imâm, the Qaramatians, and even terrorist factions like the Fatimids and Assassins. Some of these sects like the Fatimids and Qaramatians were very active in India.

With the help of the Turkish Sultans of Delhi, the missionary effort prospered, and by the end of the Mamluk Sultans, Sûfi monasteries were spread far and wide throughout the country. Aligning themselves with the already existing Muslim community of the South, they extended their influence to the Deccan and to the whole of South India.

Islam was a liberation for the lower ranks of the caste-ridden Hindu society. The Chishtya school especially, with its liberal and tolerant outlook, and emphasis on music as a means for attaining spiritual ectasy, had a great fascination for the masses. It is difficult to assess what influence these Sûfi groups exercised on the Hindu *Bhakti* movement in South India. Even if all direct influence be denied, it cannot be denied that there was a certain kindred spirit between the spirituality of the Oriental Christians, who had a strong community in South India from the early centuries of the Christian era, the mysticism of the Sûfis, and the devotionalism of the Alvars and Saivites of the Tamilnad. The political privileges, material benefits and social prestige that accompanied conversion to Islam would have been, for many, strong incentives for embracing the new faith.

The deepening opposition

By the end of the 12th century, Muslim Turks had permanently settled in large parts of Northern India and formed an important community. Though few in numbers, they were zealous in their faith, and a steady flow of conversions swelled their ranks. The Sûfis constituted a reconciling and integrating force in the community at large. But this happy situation was radically altered by the political motives of the Turkish and Mughal rulers. When they had to consolidate their conquests in the midst of a non-Islamic majority, the only way open for them was to make their initial religious aggressiveness a permanent reality. The conquerors gave expression to their contempt for the faith of the vanquished in the destruction of temples and desecration of images, and the large-scale massacre of believing Hindus. Those who did not accept death courageously were reduced to ignominious slavery. The rulers were not tolerant Sûfis, but intransigent administrators. They found the strict enforcement of Islamic law the only way to ensure a secure government. Hence, the upholding of Islamic law was more a political phenomenon than the expression of a living faith.

These Muslim rulers, acting out the role of fanatics, thereby derived the satisfaction that they were the instruments of the just punishment of God. They were stamping out idolatry, burning up by fire the thorns of the jungles of India, purifying it by the water of the sword and dissipating the vapours of infidelity, as Amir

Khusrav, one of the liberal and enlightened Muslim poets, has written.[7]

This aggressive policy of the Muslim conquerors only had the effect of totally alienating the sympathy of the Hindu community. The Hindus readily reciprocated the attitude of contempt and hatred, and isolated themselves from the alien *mlecchas* with an assumed sense of superiority. They longed for vengeance. Describing the victory of King Vijayachandra against the Muslims, the poet suggests that 'the flow of tears from the eyes of the widows of Muslim heroes (killed in battle) quenched the heat (of torment or oppression caused by the Muslims) of the world.'[8]

Thus, the Hindu-Muslim communities came to exist side by side with very little love lost between them. Al-Bîrûnî, the Muslim historian, who recorded his impressions about the Hindus with a genuine sympathy, mentions the deep difference that existed between his people and the Hindus. They differed in language, in religion and in every other respect. 'In all manners and usages they differ from us to such a degree as to frighten their children with us, with our dress, and our ways and customs, and as to declare us to be the devil's breed, and our doings as the very opposite of all that is good and proper.'[9] The caste prohibitions against outcastes were strictly enforced against the Muslims : 'They are not allowed to receive anybody who does not belong to them, even if he wished it, or was inclined to their religion. This, too, renders any connection with them quite impossible, and constitutes the widest gulf between us and them.'[10]

Hindu-Muslim encounter under Akbar the Great

A significant period of religious tolerance and of religious interaction in the long history of Hindu-Muslim confrontation came under the rule of Akbar, the Mughal Emperor. The grandchild of Baber had inherited from his two Central Asian ancestors—the Chenghis and the Timurids—a great religious flexibility of shifting easily from the Shaman cult to the Muslim Shi'a group, from Shi'a to Sunni, and from there to the mystic eclecticism of the Sûfis.

[7] *The History and Culture of Indian People,* ed. R. C. Majumdar, Vol. V, pp. 501–2.
[8] *Ibid.,* p. 502.
[9] Sachau, *Al-Biruni's India* (Bombay : Asia Publishing, 1960), pp. 17–22.
[10] Sachau, *op. cit.*

Humayun, Akbar's father, through his weakness, lost his kingdom to the Afghans, and was in exile for about fifteen years. Through the generous help of Shah Tahmasp of Persia, and under his sovereignty, Humayun had hardly succeeded in snatching back his kingdom when he died in January 1556, bequeathing his kingdom to his thirteen-year-old son Akbar. Akbar, by his military prowess and rare political wisdom, was able, within a few years, to establish his kingdom as firm and secure.

By background and upbringing, Akbar was the paragon of religious tolerance. His mother, the daughter of a Persian scholar, gave him a wide vision in matters of religion and philosophy. In his stay at the court of Kabul during his childhood, Akbar came under the influence of the holy Sûfis, expelled from Persia. These, as well as his tutor Abdul Latif, impressed on his mind the value of religious ideas which transcended sectarian barriers. His Rajput wives, too, had a softening influence on Akbar's mentality.

But more than all these, political wisdom suggested that the harmony of religions was the ideal condition for the security of such a vast kingdom. This political expediency seems, more than anything else, to have dictated Akbar's religious reactions. Placed on a tottering throne at a tender age under the threatening shadow of the Persian Shi'a Suzerainty, his means for gaining faithful Muslim followers was to live like a devout Sunni. He did this conscientiously, even humiliating himself to the extent of carrying shoes for Sadr-n-Nabi, the orthodox Sunni adviser. This fidelity to Muslim orthodoxy gave Akbar a plea to declare himself independent of the authority of the Shah of Persia, a heretic Shi'a, at the opportune moment when the powerful Shah Tahmasp was murdered in 1576 and several claimants quarrelled for succession.

In 1575, Akbar opened the *Ibadat Khana* at Fatehpur Sikri. This was a hall for religious discussions. In the beginning, participation in the discussions was restricted to the Sunni scholars, but when Akbar found that they could not agree on a satisfactory solution to the question of the number of wives he was allowed to keep, he called in the Shi'as too. These discussions showed the weakness and conflicting nature of the authorities adduced by both sides. Hence, Akbar could, without appearing an apostate, open the doors for all religions, Hindus, Parsis, Jains and Christians. In this context of general religious encounter, it became evident that the most relevant consideration was the unity and well-being of the kingdom, and the prosperity and freedom of all the people concerned.

This gave Akbar a clear pretext to shake off the legal authority of the Usmanli Khalifas of Rum, and enabled him to obtain from the principal Ulama and lawyers of Islam the *Mahazar*, or petition, of 1579. It acknowledged him the supreme arbiter within the kingdom in religious matters as well, and authorized to give out decrees in some manner based on the *Koran*.

A good many historians state that Akbar subsequently gave up the Muslim religion and founded a new religion of his own, the Din-i-Ilahi, of which he was both the temporal and spiritual head. A few assert that Din-i-Ilahi was no new religion, and that Akbar remained a Muslim till the end. But one thing is certain : Akbar did away with the privileged position of the orthodox Sunnis, and the series of regulations enacted from 1576 onwards showed a liberal trend which respected and encouraged the positive elements of all religions equally. Certain books of the Hindu scripture and the Christian Bible were ordered to be translated into Persian. Killing of animals, especially of cows, was prohibited and the royal hunt was stopped.

These regulations were a sequel to the rebellions in Bengal and Gujarat which were sponsored and planned by the Sunni Mullas. The rebellious Shaikhs and Mullas were deported and exchanged for horses. The names of Ahamad, Muhammed and Mustafa were prohibited. The study of Arabic was discouraged, and the curriculum of studies in schools was made more liberal and comprehensive than that permitted by the earlier Muslim rulers. Mosques were destroyed in centres of rebellion and new ones were prohibited to be built. The *jizya*, or special religious tax, and the pilgrim tax imposed on non-Muslims, were done away with, and the special Government allowance for Muslim pilgrims to Mecca was stopped. Brahmins were allowed to decide and settle the litigations of Hindus. Christian missionaries were allowed to build churches, preach their religion and make converts. According to Vincent A. Smith, 'The whole gist of the regulations was to further the adoption of Hindu, Jain, and Parsi practices, while discouraging or positively prohibiting essential Muslim rites.'

Several measures tended to place Akbar in the focus of religious attention. The usual *Bismilla-ir-Rahman-ir-Rahim* was replaced by the Sûfi *Allah-O-Akbar*, which had an ambiguous meaning. The same formula was to be used in greetings, instead of the *Alaikum-us-Salam*. In 1578, *sijdah*, or prostration before Akbar, was introduced as a court ceremony.

In 1581, Akbar proposed the four degrees of homage to the Emperor. This oath of fealty declared readiness to sacrifice property, life, honour, and even religion, for Akbar. He wanted his subjects to be ready to sacrifice everything for Emperor and country. Mulla Sheri could satirize these moves of Akbar thus :

> The king this year has laid claim to be a prophet;
> After the lapse of a year, please God, he will become God.

It was in 1582 that Akbar started the Din-i-Ilahi movement. Only specially chosen persons could be initiated into it, and then only by the Emperor. He used to instruct the candidates personally, test them and choose them only if they were found to be perfectly satisfactory. They were initiated on Sundays, when the Sun was up in the sky, in batches of twelve. They were given a special badge, the *Shact*, on which was engraved the Great Name, and the symbolic *Allah-O-Akbar*. In principle, it was a moral movement. The whole philosophy of the movement was set forth by Akbar in the statement : 'The pure Shact and the pure sight never err'. The moral norms were proposed in ten virtues : liberality, forgiveness, abstinence from worldly desires, freedom from the bonds of worldly existence, wisdom in devotion and meditation, prudent strength, soft voice and gentle words, equality of the brethren, perfect attachment to the Supreme Being and alienation from creatures, and dedication of the soul in love to God. Akbar was the sole priest of Din-i-Ilahi. He also encouraged the *Darshani-yas*, those subjects who had taken a vow not to take their meals without having obtained a sight of Akbar.

These moves on the part of Akbar have been interpreted in different ways by historians. Badayuni, a Sunni poet in the court of Akbar, considered Akbar an apostate from Islam, and spoke about Din-i-Ilahi as a new religion. Western historians in general have followed this view. Monserrate, Botelho and Pinheiro, who were in the court of Akbar, only suspected from these moves a desire to found a new religion of which Akbar himself would be the head. All that can be said with certainty is that Akbar wanted, besides being the Emperor, to be the spiritual guide and prophet of the people as well. Though Din-i-Ilahi has been exaggerated

as a new religion by historians, in structure it was more a religious
order like others in Sûfism, rather than a distinct sect. According to Edward S. Holden, Akbar wanted to present himself to
the people as the representative of God : 'The Sun, as the
symbol of celestial power, was worshipped daily by the ruler,
while the people saluted the Emperor as the representative of that
power on earth'.

But the spirit that inspired these revolutionary moves of Akbar
was one of tolerance for all religions. Shaikh Mubarak, a liberal
Muslim theologian, is reputed to be the originator and mainspring
of the whole plan to make Akbar the spiritual head of his people.
This liberal theology of the anti-Sunni group, which gained influence
with Akbar, provided the religious motivation for Akbar's moves
which might have only had a political aim for their immediate goal.
Akbar's religious liberalism cannot be denied on account of the
political intentions implied in it. Abdul Fazl, Akbar's favourite
poet and writer, has clearly set forth the spirit behind this liberal
outlook in a declaration which he set up in a Hindu temple in
the name of Akbar :

> O God, in every temple I see people that seek Thee,
> And in every language I hear spoken, people praise Thee!
> Polytheism and Islam feel after Thee.
> Each religion says, 'Thou art one, without equal'.
> If it be a mosque, people murmur the holy prayer,
> And if it be a Christian Church, people ring the bell from
>   love to Thee.
> Sometimes I frequent the Christian cloister, and sometimes
>   the mosque,
> But it is Thou for whom I search from temple to temple.
> Thy elect have no dealings with either heresy or orthodoxy,
> For neither of them stands behind the screen of Thy truth.

The reversal after Akbar

The atmosphere of religious liberalism and tolerance, and the
climate of religious encounter created by Akbar, did not long out-
live him. The Sunni Mullas and Shaikhs, ousted from power, felt
that their only chance for political success was in the restoration
of the privileged position of the Muslim religion. In their eyes,
Akbar had betrayed Islam. Towards the end of Akbar's reign, the
liberals lost their influence at court. Abul Fazl was murdered. A
certain Khwajah Baqi Bi-ilah, known as Khwajah Sahib, a zealous
Muslim, by his letters inspired the disgruntled Muslim leaders of

Akbar's court, and after the Emperor's death tried to influence Jahangir to restore Islam to its former hegemony. Their attempts bore fruit during the reign of Aurangazeb, who ascended the throne after ousting Darah Shiko, his brother and very tolerant towards Hindu religion. He found his best support against the Hindu Rajas in a fanatically religious Muslim group. Shaikh Ahmed Sirhindi, a convert and disciple of Khwajah Sahib, wielded his political influence at court to set the whole religious movement at the Mughal court in full reverse gear. The taxes against non-Muslims were reimposed. The Maktubat of Sirhindi, letters which he wrote to key officials in the Government for the restoration of Muslim rule, are famous for their intolerance of other religions. The Muslim scheme of education, banned by Akbar, was made obligatory again.

Thus ended the period of Hindu-Muslim religious interaction, never to return again. Under Aurangazeb, Muslim communalism increased, and in turn called for Sivaji's Maharashtra movement, which was Hindu communalism.

SIGNIFICANCE OF HINDU-MUSLIM CONFRONTATION IN INDIA

The astonishing significance of the long centuries of Hindu-Muslim co-existence in India was that nothing important came out of their encounter. Their mutual reactions were negative, rather than positive. Each underwent certain internal modifications to meet the challenges posed by the opponent. Islam had its own internal conflicts and fluctuations. Hinduism, too, had its internal rumblings. But both came out of this long religious encounter very much unchanged. After the first phase of friendly co-existence, most of the conversions from Hinduism to Islam took place, mostly under constraint.

There are several reasons for this religious immobility and antagonism. First of all, the reasons should not be sought in religion alone. There is no religion, pure and simple, in human life. Religion itself is an abstraction. The relation between man and the divine does not operate in a vacuum. Man's realization of the divine, and his creative response to it in faith, trust and self-surrender, is worked out in the concrete situations of mundane life, in which man meets with a multitude of interests.

There exist only concrete historical situations, and those who are actively involved in these situations are free human beings. It is the free choice of the individual that introduces one course of events rather than another. Hence, there are no absolutes in history. Any given set of events could have been otherwise. The liberalism of Akbar, the reaction of Khwajah Sahib and Shaikh Ahmed, and the political interests of Aurangazeb formed the Muslim community of India. If Darah Shiko had ascended the throne in the place of Aurangazeb, the later history of Hindu-Muslim relations in India would have been totally different. Hence, only in the context of individuals and their contributions can the religious phenomenon they initiated be fully understood.

On the other hand, human choice does not operate in a vacuum, and no human movement is a mere flux. There are certain regularities in human choice which the historian has to investigate, and interpret. The different concrete situations in which man exercises his free and creative response to the challenges of life may be designated, according to the different angles of vision, as cultural, social, political, economic, etc., and no one evaluation is exhaustive of the case or exclusive of other evaluations. Man's religious response is deeply bound up with these various facets of his life.

The Principle of Psychological Self-Defence : Here, the psychological dynamism, by which threatened values and traditions become rigid and unyielding in order to defend themselves, becomes apparent. Hinduism hardened itself against the threat of Islam. Muslim rulers were always considered invaders and never willingly accepted. The Holy War against all 'infidels' threatened the very existence of Hinduism. Similarly, the Sunni orthodoxy hardened its traditional position on account both of the threat posed by the religious indifference and eclecticism of Akbar, and of the tolerance of Shi'as and Sûfis who were heretics in their eyes.

This does not mean that the persons involved in these movements were all insincere, or that they did not have the best of religious motives to inspire them. Such a conclusion will not fit in with the character of Akbar, Khwajah Sahib, or Sirhindi, who were all persons of integrity and extraordinary religiosity. On the other hand, it would be quite naive to rule out human selfishness and even cold-blooded pragmatism as dominant and often decisive factors in the development of religious ideas, systems and groups. These various factors are not exclusive of each other as far as human movements are concerned, but rather complementary aspects of the same human phenomenon. The detailed medical report of a case of suicide does not exclude the moralist, the psychologist, and the sociologist from making their own independent evaluations of the case.

The East-West Confrontation : A seldom-realized fact in the interaction between Islam and Hinduism is that there was actually no encounter between them, but only a confrontation; there was no dialogue, but only two monologues. Everybody that participated in Akbar's *Ibadat Khana* seemed to be interested in teaching and proselytizing, rather than in understanding and appreciating the other's position. The study of other religions did not go much beyond translating a few texts of the other religious groups. In short, two major religious traditions—worlds apart in their approach, methodology and thought pattern—faced each other without understanding each other.

For the Greeks, and also for the Judeo-Christian and Islamic traditions which leaned heavily on their metaphysics, thought is static and exteriorized. Measurement and order occupy a central position in their mind. They seek law and neglect chance. The Hindu approach, on the other hand, is introspective, looking deep into the indefinable Self for the enduring reality in this existence of suffering. The great amount of confusion and misunderstanding brought about by the head-on confrontation of these two radically different systems of thought did not remain purely on the theoretical level, but affected every detail of popular religion.

(1) For the religions of the Judeo-Christian and Islamic traditions, there is only one God and he is the God of all. Every other god is false. Since the world belongs to God by right, the law of the one true God should be binding on everybody, whether Hindu or Muslim or Christian.

On the other hand, for the Hindu, the world is not a reality outside and separate from God, and he does not impose a law on it from the outside. The law is the *rita*, the harmony of things with the Ultimate Ground of things. Hence, the gods, avatârs and gurus are not competitors for the position of the Supreme, but are only partial manifestations of the Supreme. The more there are of them, the better can man have a choice, according to his own station and psychological condition, to understand the divine. There is no uniform and absolute law binding on everybody in the same way, but only the *svadharma*, morality proper to each individual, state, class and condition.

(2) For the West, belief in the existence of a personal God is the basic requisite of religion, and hence the atheist is the worst deviant possible, since the denial of God includes the rejection of all human values. For the Hindu, the monotheism of Islam and the Trinity of the Christians look like naive absolutizations of the particular, which may be tolerated only in the ignorant masses. Theism is only a step towards the final realization of the Absolute Consciousness, and the true religion, which is in the realization of this ultimate ground, is beyond theism. Hence, atheism is not a mere negation of God, but can be an emphatic affirmation of the ineffable Absolute.

(3) Idolatry is the greatest possible sin in the eyes of the Judeo-Christian and Islamic religions; it is a denial of the one God. On the other hand, for the Hindu, idol worship is the highest virtue, since recognizing the divine in the material realm is the highest honour he can pay to the Supreme.

(4) For the Muslim, the Jew and the Christian, scripture is the Word of God, revealing his inner secrets and law to man. As the laws established by God in nature are immutable, scripture is also unchangeable.

The Hindu position on scripture is less rigid : scriptures are the works of the sages who committed to writing their own intuition of the Absolute Reality. Though they contain the expression of the absolute order, by the very fact that they are couched in human expressions, they have only a transitory value. Even if scripture is to be taken as the word of god, it is of a god with a small letter, a god who is in relation with the world, the *Saguna Brahman*, and therefore relative and transitory. In this way, all scriptures, whether of the Hindus, or of Christians, Muslims and Parsis, have to be held in esteem, but never as absolutes.

(5) For the Muslim, the Hindu worship of the cow was rank idolatry rising out of superstition, and as such to be stamped out in all rigour, but for the Hindu, it was only part of his natural mysticism, by which he saw the whole nature of communion with the divine. The cow, on which his daily sustenance depended, was the highest symbol of beneficient nature, an expression of his optimistic outlook on nature.

From all this, it can easily be seen what a blunder it was to impose by force the whole Islamic system on India and to try to stamp out Hinduism as idolatry.

CHAPTER XII

SIKHISM

The religious movement of the Sikhs presents a unique phenomenon in the religious history of India. Started as a movement to
reconcile the two major religions of India, Hinduism and Islam, it
ended up in a new religious group, territorially, socially and politi-
cally circumscribed. Hence, it is a phenomenon, not merely in the
field of religious ideology, but more especially in the areas of
psychology, sociology and politics.

Guru Nanak is acknowledged as the founder of the Sikh religion,
but his nine successors in the office of Guru—especially Arjun
(1563–1606), a contemporary of Akbar, and Govind Singh, the last
of the Gurus—also played decisive roles in making Sikhism what it
is. But to evaluate properly the nature of the interactions which
produced Sikhism, the geographical and ethical background, and
the religious climate of the age have to be borne in mind.

The Sikh Homeland

Punjab, the homeland of the Sikhs, is the triangular Indus Plain,
made fertile by the five tributaries of the Indus, which forms the
western boundary; hence, it was called Punjab, the land of the five
rivers. It was the main gateway through which waves of different
races came into India. All the invaders naturally first settled down
in the Punjab before moving eastwards. Since the invaders seldom
brought along their wives, most of the settlers took local wives, and
the people of the Punjab became a mixture of all these invading
races along with the original settlers.

By the 15th century, the instability of constant invasions disappeared, and the people of Punjab gained a certain national consciousness with the evolution of a common tongue out of the babel
of languages brought in by the invaders. The sharp distinction of
ethnic and religious groups faded with intermarriages and the

common interest of protecting themselves and their property against future invasions.

In this evolution of Punjabi nationalism, the backbone consisted of the Jats, the peasantry of the central plains, probably of Aryan stock, who at a moment of peace migrated from the deserts of Rajasthan back to the fertile Indus Plain.

Psychologically, the Jat villages were best suited for independent religious movements : their system of village rule by an elected body of five, or *Pancâyat*, gave them a sort of semi-autonomy which the shaky rule of the invaders could not afford to violate. On the other hand, the Jats' spirit of freedom and equality rejected the Brahmanical hegemony. In fact, the Punjab always enjoyed a certain religious democracy. Hence, the *Mahabharata* pronounces an anathema on the Punjab : 'No Aryan should stay in the Punjab for even two days' (*Mahabharata*, VIII, 2063-2068). Jats, especially, conceived a condescending contempt for the Brahmin as if he were a soothsayer, and looked down on the Kshatriyas as mere mercenaries.

This amorphous, independent and nationally conscious people of the Punjab was an audience, fit not only to accept Guru Nanak's prophetic declaration : 'There is no Hindu, there is no Musalman', but also to go all the way with Guru Govind's *Khalasa,* the militant religious *élite*.

Guru Nanak

Nanak, son of Mehta Kalian Das Bedi, was born on 15 April, 1469. He was of a reflective disposition, and from his early life became intensely interested in the religious and social problems of his people. His early education introduced him to Hinduism and Islam, and he was taught both Persian and Arabic. He seems to have been greatly influenced by the devotional movements of the Muslim Sûfis as well as by the Hindu Bhaktas of his times.

A Muslim minstrel, Mardana, joined him, and they both started organizing the singing of devotional hymns among the common folk. At this early stage, Nanak is said to have received a vision in which the basic ideals of his future religious movement were given to him : *nam, dan, isnan, seva, simran*—namely, praise of the divine name, charity, ablution, service and prayer.

The Unity of God : Nanak's first move was to do away with the religious distinctions which divided the people : 'There is no

Hindu, there is no Musalman.' There is only one God, the God
of all. This faith in one God is declared in the *Japji*, the opening
hymn of the *Granth* :

> There is one God,
> He is the Supreme Truth,
> He, the Creator, is without fear and without hate,
> He, the Omnipresent, pervades the universe;
> He is not born, nor does He die to be born again.
> By His grace shalt thou worship Him,
> Before time itself, there was truth,
> When time began to run its course, He was the truth.
> Even now, He is the truth,
> And evermore shall truth prevail.

Nanak was baffled by the variety and conflicts of religious views.
Some believe in God's power, others chant his gifts and graces, yet
others his incomprehensible wisdom. Some concentrate their attention on the existence of God far away from all creation, others on
the divine presence. According to Nanak, the glorious Lord should
be smiling at this variety of human attempts to reach him. All men
live by the bounty of the Lord. Nanak loved simplicity; he wanted
to concentrate his faith on the infinite love of Truth Absolute :

> In the ambrosial hours of fragrant dawn,
> Think upon and glorify,
> His name and greatness,
> ....
> O Nanak, this alone need we know,
> That God, being Truth, is the one light of all.[1]

Nanak's basic intuition was, 'There is but one Truth, one
bestower of life'. Even if a man were to attain long life and live
through the four *yugas*, and yet be without the grace of God, he
would be disowned in God's presence.

In Nanak, the original simplicity of Indian piety, so well illus-
trated in the Indus Valley religious culture and in Dravidian
devotionalism, reasserted itself against the formalism of the Brahmins and the organized religion of the Muslim Mullas. God 'cannot
be installed like an idol, nor can man shape his likeness,' said
Nanak. Hearken to the Name of the Supreme; in simple, loving

---

[1] *Sâcâ Sâhib Sâc nâe Bhâkhyâ bhâu apâr, Selections from the Sacred
Writings of the Sikhs,* UNESCO Collection (London: Allen & Unwin, 2nd
imp., 1965), p. 31.

devotion place all trust in God; sing his praises in unity and harmony with other men—such was the substance of Nanak's instructions. Simple openness to the grace of God is what is implied by 'hearkening to the Name'. Through faith in the Divine Name, man can obtain the godliness of Siva, Brahma and Indra, said Nanak; he can thereby learn the art of Yoga, and imbibe the whole Vedic wisdom,[2] and reach the final enlightenment in which the whole universe stands self-revealed.[3]

Guru Nanak's religion is characteristic of the troubled times in which he lived. Ordinary people could not place their trust in external authority and institutional religion. Everything was in confusion, and the very institutions which had to provide the security and guidance for the common man were struggling to preserve their own existence. People had only their inner light to show them the right path, and only a pure conscience for spiritual guarantee. Pilgrimages, penances and other observances had lost their religious meaning and became mere customs. Hence, Nanak declared them to be of little merit. One who hears, believes and loves the Name has a place of pilgrimage within him, and he shall bathe and be made clean. The Pandits, the Qazis and the Yogis know nothing about the mystery of creation; God alone, who made it, knows it.[4]

Donning a peculiar pilgrim garb, a combination of the dress of the Hindu Sadhu and of the Muslim Fakir, Nanak made an extensive tour of all the famous holy places of both Hindus and Muslims. He first went eastwards to the Hindu *tirthas* of Mathura, Benares, Gaya, up to Assam, returning by the south through Puri, Malabar, Konkan, Bombay and Rajasthan, then north to the Himalayan regions, and finally west to the Muslim holy places of Mecca and Medina, and up to Baghdad. Everywhere he preached the unity of God and the unity of all religions, and tried to impress on the

---

[2] *Sunîai îsar barmâ ind., Ibid.,* p. 33.

[3] *Manain surt hovai man budh., Ibid.,* p. 35.

[4] *Tirath tap dayâ dat dân, Ibid.,* p. 40. Cf. Dorothy Field, *The Religion of the Sikhs* (London: John Murray, 1914): 'It is a pure lofty monotheism, which sprang out of an attempt to reform and to simplify Muhammadanism and Hinduism, and which, though failing in this attempt, succeeded in binding together, like Judaism of old, a whole race in a new bond of religious zeal.' Cf. also Frederic Pincott, *Sikhism in its Relation to Muhammadanism* (London: W. H. Allen & Co., 1885): '. . . the religion of Nanak was really intended as a compromise between Hinduism and Muhammadanism, if it may not even be spoken of as the religion of a Mohammadan sect.'

common people the futility of ceremonial worship, which he designated as false and superstitious. He is said to have demonstrated one day the uselessness of offering water of the holy river to the dead, by pretending to splash up water from the Ganges to his dry farm hundreds of miles away. Similarly, he tried to show the unreasonableness of localized worship: to the Mulla who remonstrated with him about his sleeping with his feet towards the Ka'ba, he said: 'Then turn my feet towards some direction where there is no God, nor the Ka'ba.'

The Community of the Disciples: Nanak's main goal was to fight the evils of caste and class and build up a community open to all men. So, at an early stage in his religious movement, he instituted the *sangat* and the *pangat*, the mixed community of disciples gathered at the feet of the Guru, and the community kitchen, where all sat in the same row (*pangat*) for meals, regardless of class distinctions. Participation in the common meal was made the condition for hearing the words of the Guru.

Nanak's religion was that of the common man. According to him, religion had to be lived in the midst of the common people, ministering to their needs and facing their problems. Hence, he had no esteem for the *siddhas* and *yogis* who forsook the world, oblivious of their social duties and obligations to their fellow men: 'The earth is all seized by sin. The accomplished saints and sages, the *siddhas*, are hiding themselves in the recesses of mountains. Who is there to save the world?' he complained. This social concern of Baba Nanak caught fire when, in 1521, Baber laid waste Saidpur and massacred the people. After describing the sad plight of the people, he rebukes the Lodhi Sultans of Delhi for not defending their subjects: 'The dogs (Lodhis) have thrown away the priceless inheritance; when they are dead and gone, no one will remember them with regard.'

As a popular leader, Nanak emphasized the role of the Guru in the community. The institution of the Guru, or teacher, was held in veneration, both by the Hindus, and by the Muslims of Persia and Afghanistan, and especially by the Shi'as and Sûfis. *Sikh* means *sishya*, or disciple, and the Sikh religion is the community of the disciples. As Sher Singh says, 'the belief of unity in the plurality of the gurus served a useful purpose in the development of Sikhism. But for this belief, there would have been no Sikh nation.'

According to Nanak, without the Guru there could be no salvation.

> The word of the Guru is the inner music,
> The word of the Guru is the highest Scripture;
> The word of the Guru is all-pervading.
> The Guru is Siva, the Guru is Vishnu and Brahma,
> The Guru is the Mother Goddess.[5]

However, the Guru is only a guide, not a god nor a prophet : 'At God's gate there is no room for a prophet,' Nanak told a Muslim. A Guru is to be consulted, not to be worshipped. All the same, he is a necessary guide :

> As a team of oxen are we driven,
> By the ploughman, our Teacher,
> By the furrows made are thus writ
> Our actions—on the earth our paper.

Nanak did not want to found a distinct religious group; it only evolved by dint of circumstances. When Nanak went to visit Multan, the city chief sent out a delegation to meet him at the gate with a cup brimful of milk, implying that the place was filled with religions and that they needed no new one there. Nanak sent back the cup, placing a jasmine flower over the milk. His meaning was that he did not intend to found any new religion, but only to add a little jasmine fragrance to the already existing milk of religion. But the religious movement he started developed into a distinct social and religious group, even during his lifetime. Nanak's insistence on *sat-sang*, truthful companionship, became in practice the community of those who accepted him as their Guru.

The break with the communities of Muslims and Hindus was implicit in the teaching of Nanak himself; he rejected both the Muslim Prophet and the Hindu gods. He avoided the Arabic language of the Muslims and the Sanskrit of the Hindus and wrote his hymns in the popular Punjabi, thereby restricting his teaching to the Punjabi-speaking area of the Indus Valley. The centre at Kartarpur where Nanak spent his last years, and where large crowds of his disciples gathered together to hear him, became the new centre of religious gathering for the Sikhs. The community kitchens, or *Guru ka langar*, set up in various parts of the country naturally became rallying points for the Sikhs. Going to eat with these mixed

[5] *Adi Granth,* trs. Ernest Trumpp (London, 1877), Japji 5.

groups naturally meant a break with orthodox religious tradition.

The doctrinal synthesis between Hinduism and Islam was a more important factor in isolating the Sikhs as a religious group. Nanak accepted such elements as he thought useful for the particular social and historical situation from both Hinduism and Islam. On the one hand, he accepted from Hinduism the idea of God as the all-embracing reality with a 'million eyes, a million forms and a million feet', and yet formless; he also accepted the practice of reciting the Divine Names, followed by the Hindu *Bhaktas* for concentrating their attention on the Divine Reality. But, on the other hand, his conception of God as father, lover, master, Great Giver, and above all, True Creator (*sat Kartar*), approached closer to the Judeo-Christian and Islamic modes of thought than to the Hindu. For Nanak, the Divine Name was not merely a means for concentrating attention, a designation of the ineffable, but was the symbol of the Supreme Person.

> The Lord is the Truth Absolute,
> True is His Name.
> His language is love infinite;
> His creatures ever cry to Him.
> ....
> Priceless are His attributes,
> Priceless His dealings;
> Priceless the stores of His virtues,
> Priceless the dealers in them.
> ....
> Pricelessly precious is devotion to Thee,
> Pricelessly precious is absorption in Thee,
> Priceless His law and spirit of righteousness.

He accepted the Hindu doctrine of transmigration of souls, but his conception of the moral order was that of the law set out by the Supreme Person. His denial of both the Koran and the Veda, the rejection of the services of both the Muslim Mulla and the Brahmin, the repudiation of both the Islamic legal system and of the symbolism of Hindu ritual, all these isolated the adopted ideas from their original sources. This also had the result of closing the door on any elaboration or deepening of the adopted ideas, because normal constant recourse to their traditional sources was prevented. On the other hand, this helped the movement not to get lost in philosophical and theological speculations, but to concentrate its attention entirely in the problems and needs of the common man.

Sikhism grew up as a religion of the common man, and its evolution was on the social and political planes.

THE SUCCESSORS OF NANAK

The growth of the Sikh movement under the nine Gurus who followed Nanak was mainly in social and political directions : more centres were built, the community of the disciples was organized, and new cities were founded. Under Guru Arjun, Amritsar was built as a centre of pilgrimage, with its golden temple a parallel to Benares for the Hindus and to Mecca for the Muslims. When Arjun died under torture, a victim to the suspicions of Jehangir, Hargobin, his successor, found it necessary to protect the new religious group with arms. With the formation of the Sikh army, the Guru had to take on the role of a military leader, too. He became the Sat Padasha, true Emperor.

Spiritual and temporal administration could not go together; quarrels of succession disrupted the community, so Guru Gobind, who had to maintain his position against the crafty and ruthless Aurangazeb by political diplomacy and military strength, finally found it best to leave the spiritual guidance of the people to the *Granth Sahib*, the book of the writings of earlier Gurus, and to the Sangh, the community which assembled only at certain times. His successors were political leaders, going to the extreme, sometimes, of bandits like Banda, and showing real statesmanship at times, like Ranjit Singh.

To an outsider, this later development of Sikhism may appear a distortion of the ideals of Nanak, a deviation of the movement itself, the result of over-systematization and reification of religion. But the Sikhs find a religious unity in the historical movement of their nation. As Ganda Singh says: 'The period of the Gurus was that of the education of the Sikhs in the light of the Master's teachings, and it aimed at so moulding their lives as to develop them into men with unflinching faith in God and selfless devotion to the service of humanity. Their transformation to a militant people grew out of their will to resist evil and tyranny and to make human life worth living, free of fear and enmity.'

CHAPTER XIII

CHRISTIANITY AND THE HINDU-CHRISTIAN ENCOUNTER

CHRIST AND THE CHRISTIAN WORLD VIEW

Christianity is Christ. This is quite obvious, for if there is anything unique that distinguishes Christianity from other religions, it is the historical personality of Christ, his teaching, and his redemptive work in the name of humanity. The present Christian era computes the years roughly from the birth of Christ, and the years before him are counted backwards. Coming at a definite point in the history of the human race, he combined in his truly divine personality a perfect human nature and the true divinity. In his life and works he showed himself one single 'I'—at the same time fully man and also really God.

Christianity is based on the supposition that the whole human race is a single family with a single history, seriously damaged by an initial revolt against God its Creator. However, at a specific point in its history, a Divine Person, the Son of God, enters humanity, assuming to himself a perfect human nature, being born as Jesus of human history: by his suffering and death on the cross at the supereminent position of the Son of God and by the all-influencing power of his divinity, he summarized in himself, in a way, the whole of human history: by his suffering and death on the cross at the hands of the Jews, he satisfied for all the sins of humanity, repaired it as a living organism and reconstituted it as a new family.

Hence, Christ and his redeeming work in the name of all men belong to human history and to all men by right. The Gospel, or the Good News, which he committed to his disciples to be preached to all men everywhere, is that he has achieved in himself the salvation of all men. In Christ, divinity and humanity are reconciled; human nature has gone beyond all the limitations of the relative world and has touched the Absolute in the truly divine personality of the Son. Hence, to attain God, men have only to unite themselves to Christ, the new head and vivifying centre of humanity. This is to be done through faith and through integration to the Church, which is the community of the disciples of Christ.

Jesus Christ did not propose his teaching as an abstract doctrine. He gathered around him a community of disciples, who were the immediate witnesses of his personality, teaching, suffering, death and resurrection. This living historical experience of what is designated as 'the Christ-event' is the beginning of Christianity. This community of disciples communicated their experience to others, and so the original small gathering soon expanded into the Church. When the Church extended far and wide, the original Christ-experience had to be committed to writing as the authentic preaching. The Gospels written by Matthew, Mark, Luke and John constitute the substance of the apostolic preaching on Christ. The books of the Old Testament, which Christ declared he came to fulfil and complete, the writings of the Apostles on the matter of their preaching, and the four Gospels, make up Christian scripture, the Bible.

Christianity is, therefore, a historical religion. Only by a living experience-integration in the Christian community, which maintains historical continuity with the original community of the immediate disciples of Christ, can one adequately and properly attain Christ. The four Gospels are history, but they are not chronicles, nor do they propose to present a biography of Christ. They are history in the sense that they proclaim the meaning of the Christ-event for all men who are willing to believe and accept the message of salvation. Thus, St Mark presents us with 'the Good News of Jesus Christ, the Son of God' (Mk 1, 1) in order to emphasize the divinity of Christ and the supernaturality of the truth he proclaimed, neither of which fall under sense observation. Christ, for Mark, is the Son of God who has come as the Servant of the Lord (Is 42, 1) 'to lay down his life as a ransom for all the rest of men' (Mk 10, 45; Is 53, 5–8). According to Matthew, the dominant note in the Christ-event is the restoration of the rule of God over humanity; God is the true Emmanuel, residing with men. In Luke, Jesus is primarily the Saviour who presents the divine response to the religious aspirations of humanity typified in the yearnings of the Hellenic tradition. John, on the other hand, at the same time as flaunting his concrete experience of the Word of Life (1 Jn 1, 1–3), loves to contemplate Christ, the Word of God that illumines every man that comes into the world.

Thus, Christianity presents a historical view of the human race and of the whole world. But this history, centred in Christ, becomes the sacred story of God's saving self-manifestation in the one 'Word-made-flesh', fulfilling all the deep-rooted aspirations of man, and constituting humanity into a single family, a single living organism. The Son of God became the son of man so that the sons of men might become the sons of God in that one Son. He is the unique head and source of life; all men are to be his living members. He is the vine, and every member of humanity is a branch, drawing life and fruitfulness from the vine.

This sense of the oneness of all men in Christ, the Son of God, urged the Christian community to spread the Word to every corner of the world, and to make its presence felt in every country in order to impart to others the unique experience it gained from the historical Christ.

CHRISTIANITY IN INDIA

The Christian community in India is almost as ancient as Christianity itself. The Gospel was preached in India by the immediate disciples of Christ, by St Thomas the Apostle, and probably also by St Bartholomew the Apostle. Though the traditions concerning this apostolic preaching were sometimes questioned by critical historians, present-day scholarship is strongly inclined to accept their veracity. The strongest argument in favour of the tradition, especially about the preaching of St Thomas in India, is that the origin of this tradition is not in India but outside, like the Acts of Thomas composed in the Middle East, and the testimonies of Pantenus, St Ephrem, and other impartial witnesses. In any case, nobody questions the existence of a strong Christian community in India from the early centuries of the Christian era. Cosmas Indicopleustes in the sixth century speaks of Christian communities well established in Kerala, Kalyan and other places. Copper plates granting privileges to the Christians and dating from around the ninth century or even earlier have been discovered. Several Persian crosses with inscriptions in Pahlavi have been found in Kerala and Madras. All this presents archaeological evidence of the early existence of Christian communities in India.

In the Middle Ages, Marco Polo, the Venetian traveller (1293), the Franciscan friar John de Monte Corvino (1292–93), the Dominican Jordan of Toulouse (1302), and John Marignolli who was sent by the Pope (1348) present consistent testimony that the Christians had established themselves as respected citizens, prominent both in business and military service.

Christians and Indian community

The Christians in the Malabar coast were accepted without difficulty into the caste structure of the community, and had a position similar to that of the Brahmins. Seven Brahmin families, said to have been converted by St Thomas the Apostle, supplied priests for the Christian community, while in practical life, Christians were considered equals and brothers in arms with the Nairs. Christians kept the social customs and practices according to their ancient Hindu tradition without any prejudice to their new faith. As to religious practices like family prayers, church attendance, observance of festivals and personal devotions, there was very little to distinguish between Hindus and Christians, except that one group frequented temples while the others had their churches. There was close co-operation between church and temple on the popular level in the observance of festivals.

There was little scope for dialogue or confrontation on the doctrinal level. Christians had no theologians of any note among them since they were administered by Bishops sent from Mesopotamia, and these pastors cared little for theoretical discussions and religious disputations. On the side of the Hindus, the Brahmin scholars were a small minority and they kept their discussions to themselves and would not condescend to communicate their wisdom to the unintelligent masses. Besides, the common Christian folk did not present any challenge to the Hindus. The Hindu Rajas, who had unquestioned power in the whole region, considered it their duty to protect the weaker community of the Christians. Hindu scholars like Sri Sankaracharya had their hands full fighting the Buddhists and Jains, who were the real enemies of Hinduism. Hence, what we find is a happy co-existence of Hindus and Christians, with a certain community of life on the socio-political and cultural levels. When, in the eighth century, the Muslims came to the Malabar coast, they also integrated themselves into the social set-up, until the time Islam became a political force in the north.

The coming of the Portuguese

With the arrival of Vasco da Gama in Calicut in 1498, the Christian situation was somewhat changed. The Christians felt a certain kinship with the newcomers on account of the community of faith, and sought protection from them against the Saracens who were a constant threat to the Christians' trade in pepper and other spices.

The Portuguese, on the other hand, were ambitious, and fought not only the Arab pirates, but also the Hindu kings who did not side with the Portuguese. They had very little understanding of the religions of the new peoples they met with. Everything they did not understand they branded as idolatry and superstition. The memory of the Crusades in the Middle East was still vivid. Peter Alvares Cabral started from Lisbon in March, 1500, with a fleet of thirteen ships. Sending them off, the king exhorted them to spread the Christian faith and religion in those distant lands and also 'to take up a just and holy war against the wicked enemies of Christ'.[1] This added a fanatic fervour to the adventurist spirit of the sailors and urged them on to all kinds of rash and imprudent acts. In Calicut, they antagonized the Zamorin, and tried the generosity and loyalty of the King of Cochin to the extreme through the unnecessary wars they incited. They did everything to westernize the Christians of Kerala, endeavoured to change their age-old customs and traditions, did away with the oriental Bishops who ruled over the Kerala Church, and got Portuguese Bishops appointed in their place, and so totally alienated the sympathy of Indian Christians. This aversion for the Portuguese came to a climax when, in 1653, a good section of the Malabar Christians took an oath at the Cross of Mattancherry, Cochin, never again to accept a Portuguese Bishop as their pastor.

In Goa, the Portuguese ordered all Hindus in the port area either to become Christians or to vacate the place. Temples were closed and their properties confiscated, and a number of forced conversions are reported in the complaints submitted by the aggrieved parties to the Pope in Rome. The zealous missionaries

[1] Joannis Petri Maffei, S.J., *Historiarum Indicarum,* Lib. XVI (Coloniae Agrippinae, 1589), p. 29: 'Huic ab Rege mandatum in primis, ut Christianam fidem, religionemque in iis regionibus tum serere, tum amplificare omni studio insisteret, dein . . . cumque nefariis Christi hostibus justum piumque susciperet bellum.'

who accompanied the sailors were often forced to be instruments and agents of the ambitious political power.

But there were a great many holy men, like St Francis Xavier and Friar Vincent, who courageously withstood the political pressures and dedicated their whole lives to the service of the poor people on the Western coast. But these did not have the preparation nor opportunity to enter into any real dialogue with the Hindus. In preaching the Christian Gospel to the poor, they relied on the standard catechism of the West and simple apologetics.

A notable exception was Robert de Nobili, S.J. (1577–1656), an Italian nobleman who, adopting the way of life of a Hindu *sanyasin*, tried to communicate the Christian message in Hindu style and terminology to the Hindu intelligentsia in the mission of Madura. He had a sincere love for the Hindus and often spoke highly of Hindu philosophy.

Even he was unable to initiate any real dialogue with Hinduism. He adopted Hindu style and terminology purely as a method of approach, and not for any real admiration for Hindu tradition : 'To attack from the front would be to close all doors of access; not because these false idols were not worthy of all opprobrium but for the sake of the salvation of souls.'[2] His apologetics, detailed in his *Jnanopadesa Kurippidam*, first explain the tests to distinguish the true religion from the false. Applying these to Hinduism, he concludes : 'When we consider what is going on in these temples, the nude idols on the *gopurams*, and the *ther*, and the dance, fun and frivolity of the *devadasis*, and the many opportunities for the worshipper to sin with them . . . we can say there is no chance of leaving one's sin and doing good.'[3]

De Nobili's methods of adaptation to Indian culture were partially successful, but they were severely objected to by those in the West and were discontinued.

Portuguese missionaries extended their activities even outside the Portuguese dominions. They gained admission to the Mughal court and Akbar permitted them to preach the Gospel, make converts and build churches. Jesuit missions existed in the Mughal Empire, though in a weak condition, even after the death of Akbar, under Jehangir and Aurangazeb. Father Antony de Andrade even

[2] Quoted in J. S. Chandler, *History of the Jesuit Mission in Madura* (Madras, 1909), p. 30.
[3] *Jnanopadesa Kurippidam*, p. 26.

made an adventurous journey to Tibet *via* Badrinath in 1624, reached the town of Tsaparang in the Upper Sutlej, preached to the king and queen of the region through an interpreter, and established a mission there. After the Jesuits were banished from the Portuguese dominions in 1759, the missions were taken over by the Carmelites and Capuchins. They continued the missionary work in centres like Marwar, Jaipur, Agra and Delhi.

But in terms of a real religious dialogue, the net result of the Portuguese encounter with India was rather negative. When they succeeded in creating a few pockets of Christianity like Goa, in so doing, they closed all avenues of religious encounter with the rest of the population of India. By the middle of the 17th century, the Portuguese were defeated by the Dutch and ousted from their possessions, except for a few isolated places like Goa, Daman and Diu.

The Dutch apologetics

The Dutch missionaries took over the place of the Portuguese in the work of evangelization, but their method of approach to Hinduism and Islam was no different from that of their predecessors. *Thirty-four conferences between the Danish Missionaries and the Malabarian Brahmas (or Heathen Priests) in the East Indies, Concerning the Truth of the Christian Religion, Together with Some Letters Written by the Heathens to the Said Missionaries*, translated from the High Dutch by M. Philips, and printed in London in 1719, gives us some idea of their religious dialogue. The missionary starts giving a positive exposition of the Christian doctrine, existence of one God, his act of creation and providence for men, sin of man, and the Divine Incarnation to save men, and the rest. But this exposition evokes this response from the Brahmin :

> I believe all you say of God's dealings with you white Europeans to be true, but his appearances and Revelations among us Black Malabarians have been quite otherwise. And the Revelations he made of himself in this land are as firmly believed here to be true, as you believe those made in your country, for, as Christ in Europe was made man, so here our God Wischtnu was born among us Malabarians. And as you hope for salvation through Christ, so we hope for salvation through Wischtnu. And to save you one way, and us another, is one of the pastimes and diversions of Almighty God (p. 14).

The missionary's next step was to go to a Hindu temple and point out all the abuses that went on there, the greed of the priests, the immoral life of the temple prostitutes, and so on. The whole method consists in a comparison of the tenets and practices of the two religions in order to show the superiority of one's own religion.

Coming of the British and the progress of Christian missions

When the British East India Company gained a foothold in India in the 18th century, no Christian missionary was granted licence to reside in the Company's settlements. However, the arrival in 1793 of William Carey, a zealous English missionary, opened a new chapter in the Christian encounter with India. Though he, too, was fired with a zeal for preaching the Gospel and converting the 'heathens' to the faith,[4] he had a positive appreciation of the non-Christian religions. Instead of engaging in futile and negative criticism of religions other than Christianity, he did pioneer work to translate the Bible into Indian languages, and to start schools to educate children.

Educational enterprise

Through pressure exerted in the British Parliament and by public opinion, the East India Company lifted the ban on missionaries at the time of the revision of its Charter in 1813. The Charter made a new provision that a sum of £10,000 be set aside annually by the Company for native education, oriental and occidental. Serampore College, founded by Carey in 1818 for the promotion of 'piety and learning', was the beginning of an apostolate which marked the specific line of Christian contribution to India. Long before this, in the 16th century, Friar Vincent had founded and conducted a school for the Malabar Christians at Cranganore, and the Jesuits continued this educational apostolate at Vaipikkotta. But these and St Paul's College at Goa, founded by the Portuguese, only emphasized the teaching of Christian religion and the training of Christian missionaries. With Carey, this endeavour expanded into the field of general education open to all, irrespective of caste and creed. This Christian endeavour gained momentum with Lord Macaulay's *Minute* of 1835, outlining a policy of imparting English

---

[4] Cf. William Carey, *An Enquiry into the Obligations of Christians to use Means for the Conversion of Heathens* (London, 1792, reprinted 1961).

education in schools and colleges, and a number of colleges sprang up under Christian sponsorship, like the Madras Christian College, Wilson College (Bombay), St Xavier's College (Calcutta), St John's College (Agra), Ewing Christian College (Allahabad), and American College (Madura). This educational enterprise evolved into a vast network of institutions of different levels and scopes. According to the Catholic Directory of India, 1969, there were, under Catholic ownership and management, 110 colleges, 183 technical institutes, 74 training institutions, 1,198 secondary schools, and 7,042 primary and middle schools. Almost an equal number of institutions are conducted under the auspices of the National Christian Council.

This concern with general education indicates an area of specific Christian contribution to the Indian community. Indeed, for a country which prides itself on the memory of the ancient world-famous centres of learning like Nalanda and Taxila, the enterprise of public education was nothing new. But, owing to the repressive and restrictive policies of the Muslim rulers through several centuries, Hindu enthusiasm for higher educational institutions was stifled for generations. Muslims in general lacked a tradition of higher learning. To this situation of almost general illiteracy, the Christian missionaries came, from a background of several centuries of high literacy and university learning, open to all. Hence, it was only natural that they should concentrate their attention, above all, to the removal of illiteracy through an adequate school system.

Social services

Another area where the Christian contribution made a beneficial impact on Indian life was that of health services and other social activities. India's ancient Ayurvedic and other medical traditions had become almost obsolete and inefficient, owing to the lack of fresh research, want of provision for the training of personnel on a massive scale, and refusal to employ efficient modern methods. Advanced Western medical treatment was a luxury open only to the wealthy. Christian missionaries, coming from a background of advanced medical facilities, tried to make them available to the common people. Hence, alongside Christian Missions, hospitals, nursing homes and dispensaries were started. Similarly, homes for the aged and abandoned, orphanages, and a number of other specialized institutions for the service of the weak and ailing members of the society, became the expressions of Christian love for all men.

MODERNIZATION AND WESTERNIZATION

The immediate effect of this encounter with the West was an all-out effort for modernization, but it carried with it the undesirable side effect of Westernization. The advent of the Europeans on the Indian coast was the demonstration of superior scientific discoveries and technological achievement which could not fail to impress the Indian masses. When they got a chance to enjoy the amenities of life brought about by such progress, there was evidently great admiration for the people who enjoyed those things and also a strong urge to imitate them.

After Britain had imposed its rule and law over the whole Indian sub-continent and peace was established, the wealthier classes made it their ambition to visit England and, if possible, to have their children educated in the West. Motilal Nehru counted it a great achievement to have attained a certain equality with the English middle class and to have provided all his children with a Western education. Mahatma Gandhi, in his earlier years, took pride in his English education and imposed Western customs and manners on his whole household, until he was inspired with the urge to launch the freedom fight against the Western powers in South Africa and India. The father of Sri Aurobindo Ghosh was very insistent that his son should not take anything from the Indian tradition, but should get his whole education in England. The wealthier folk in Bombay and Calcutta had adopted the Western manner of living by the early nineteenth century.

The Christian missionaries were already unconsciously fostering this trend towards Westernization in the sixteenth century. In baptizing Indians, they wanted to give them the best they could, and often even gave them Portuguese and Spanish family names. They must also have felt that a thorough break with one's cultural past was the best guarantee of sincerity and firmness of conversion, so conversion to Christianity was often associated by the Hindus with wearing trousers, drinking alcohol, smoking cigarettes and eating meat. In a talk given in Bangalore in 1927, Mahatma Gandhi told the Christian missionaries :

Whilst a boy, I heard it said that to become a Christian was to have a brandy bottle in one hand and beef in the other. Things

are better now, but it is not unusual to find Christianity synony-
mous with denationalization and Europeanization.[5]

There was no lack of Portuguese and British politicians who
thought it an advantage to form Christians into a culturally
Westernized group as a reliable support for their political interests,
but Westernization was not restricted to Christians. Even after
Independence, status-seeking high caste Hindus continue to emulate
the Europeans in their mode of life, while the lower strata of society
emulate the higher castes.

RENASCENT HINDUISM

On the other hand, the influence of Western Christianity initiated
a move towards the reformation of Hindu customs and traditions.
Raja Rammohan Roy, Swami Dayananda Saraswati, Kesab
Chandra Sen, Swami Vivekananda and other enlightened Hindus
spoke out strongly against polytheism, superstition, prohibitions
against sea travel and other abuses that existed in the Hindu community. Rammohan Roy, for example, in his writings referred to
the palliative way in which Europeans tried to understand Hindu
idol worship in the right sense and said that actually 'the Hindus
today believe in the existence of innumerable gods and goddesses'
distorting thereby 'the allegorical adoration of the true Deity'.[6]

Deeply affected by the social evils of the Indian community,
some of these Hindu reformers were greatly attracted to the teachings of Christ. In 1820, Rammohan Roy published *The Precepts of
Jesus, The Guide to Peace and Happiness*, a collection of words of
Jesus in the order in which they are found in the synoptic Gospels
with Bengali and Sanskrit translations.[7] He prayed for the day
'when everyone will regard the Precepts of Jesus as the sole guide
to peace and happiness'.[8] He was also the founder of the *Brahma
Samaj*, which endeavoured to purify Hinduism of all superstitions
and to form a kind of unified universal religion that would combine
the good elements of all religions. This movement later gained the

[5] Mahadev Desai in *Young India*, 11–8–1927, quoted in M. K. Gandhi,
Christian Missions, Their Place in India (Ahmedabad, 1941), p. 160.
[6] *Translation of Several Principal Books, Passages and Texts of the
Vedas* (London: Parkay, Allen & Co., 1832), Introduction, p. 4.
[7] *English Works of Raja Rammohan Roy*, ed. Kalidas Nag and Debaiyoti
Burwan (Calcutta, 1946), Vol. V, 5ff.
[8] *Ibid.*, Vol. VI, p. 93.

ardent support of Debendranath Tagore and of Kesab Chandra
Sen. But it split up into several groups, Kesab himself becoming the
founder of a group styled The New Dispensation!

These efforts at reform, inspired by the encounter with
Christianity, produced a new outlook in Hinduism itself. As D. S.
Sarma states in *Renascent Hinduism*,[9] Hinduism no longer objected
to foreign travel or to dining with people of other castes and races.
Women were emancipated. The most important change was that
the caste system, supported even with texts from the Vedas, 'is
tottering to its fall along with its ugly pendant—the system of
outcastes'.

Spirit of Social Service : This renascence of Hinduism did not
only do away with the defects of superstition and social bigotry;
it also introduced new outlooks and orientations in tune with the
needs of modern times. A sense of urgency for service to the poor
was one of the new attitudes. As Gandhi confesses, he went to
South Africa 'for travel, for finding an escape from Kathiawad
intrigues and for gaining my own livelihood'. But there he found
himself entirely absorbed in the service of the community. Gandhiji
even started exhorting the Christian missionaries to identify with
the Indian masses : 'You cannot present the hungry and famished
masses with God. Their God is their food.'[10] Sri Vinoba Bhave,
Sri Jayaprakash Narayan and a good many other leaders have
dedicated their lives to the service of the poor and needy, in order
to bring about social equality among the masses of India. They
have also proclaimed a *loknîti*, social righteousness, based on respect
for the life and personality of others, recognition of others' rights
and abandonment of all exploitation.

Religious Tolerance : Tolerance of all religions is a principle
which has assumed the stature of a philosophy in this new encounter of faiths. Sri Vivekananda bore the torch of tolerance to
the Parliament of Religions in Chicago. Scholars like Dr S. Radhakrishnan and Sri Vivekananda appealed to the basic unity of all
religions as the reason for tolerance. For Mahatma Gandhi, the basis
of religious tolerance is this : 'All faiths constitute a revelation of
Truth, but all are imperfect, and liable to error.'[11] In a discussion

[9] D. S. Sarma, *Renascent Hinduism* (Bombay: Bharatiya Vidya Bhavan,
1966), pp. 3–4.
[10] *Young India*, 9–8–1925.
[11] From *Yervada Mandir*, Ch. X, quoted in *Christian Missions*, p. 3.

with the missionaries of Bangalore in 1927, Gandhi insisted on the principle of religious dialogue :

> To you who have come to teach India, I therefore say, you cannot give without taking. If you have come to give rich treasures of experiences, open your hearts out to receive the treasures of this land, and you will not be disappointed; neither will you have misread the message of the Bible.[12]

Ecumenism within Hinduism : A feature closely allied to this new awareness of religious tolerance is the admission of those lower or animistic forms of religious cult prevalent in villages as forms of Hinduism. 'Hinduism is a league of religions.'[13] The innumerable sects and groups differ vastly from place to place in their beliefs and practices, though they may all be grouped loosely under the main sectarian forms of Vaishnavism, Saivism and Saktiism. In the fight for Independence, Indian leaders like Mahatma Gandhi, Aurobindo Ghosh and others realized that any revival of political consciousness should have a strong religious tone, which was the main strength of India's tradition. They also realized that any revival of popular Hinduism would mean the resurgence of local cults and the breaking up of the Hindu community into innumerable warring factions. So, at the same time as preaching a religious revival, they tried to steer it away from traditional popular lines, from caste and untouchability, sectarianism and bigotry. A number of legislative measures taken, especially after the independence of India in 1947, like the opening of Hindu temples to Harijans or low castes and the strict prohibition of caste discriminations, were all aimed at 'catholicizing' Hinduism.

Gita and Revival : The great importance *Bhagavad Gita* has gained as *the* Gospel of Hinduism is symbolic of this catholic spirit. *Gita* does not belong to the Sruti, or scripture proper. It is not even *smriti*, the commentary literature immediately following scriptures. In origin it is a sectarian book. However, it presents a wonderful synthesis among the various schools and systems of Hinduism —a reconciliation between Vedântic absolutism and Sâmkhya-Yoga dualism : between the abstract mysticism and fire sacrifice of the Vedic tradition on the one hand, and the intensely personalistic and sentimental devotionalism of the Agamas. Besides this, *Gita* emphasizes a number of values very important in modern times.

[12] *Young India*, 11–8–1927, quoted in *Christian Missions*, p. 159.
[13] D. S. Sarma, *op. cit.*, p. 3.

(1) *Svadharma and Personal Freedom* : *Gîta's* message of *svadharma*, the personal duty of disinterested action, goes a long way towards emphasizing the freedom and responsibility of the individual in a democratic society. In recent times, there is greater emphasis on what is called caste-spirit, in opposition to the caste-structure. The arrogance and vested interests of privileged castes, along with the slavish mentality of the underprivileged castes and outcastes, are strenuously fought against. This is the corrupt caste-structure which has outlived its usefulness. On the other hand, in a free society, each individual has his position and particular responsibility. In the *Gîta*, the fault of Arjuna is that he is hesitant before his duty, carried away by his feeling for kith and kin. Sri Krishna urges him to fight because, as a Kshatriya commissioned to fight and uphold righteousness, he has to fulfil that obligation with a disinterested and selfless devotion to duty.

Mahatma Gandhi expanded this devotion to duty into a social commitment, drawing inspiration from Ruskin's *Unto This Last*, which he translated under the title *Sarvodaya*, 'welfare of all'. Only in achieving the welfare of all, can the individual attain his own welfare. Whatever work one does in one's station in life is as good as any other profession, so long as the individual makes his contribution to society.

(2) *Ideal of Action* : If the Hindu theory of *Karma Samsâra* was often misunderstood as being an indication of a pessimistic outlook on life and of a world-denying attitude, contemporary mentality has shifted the emphasis to the *Gîta* ideal of action. The Lord in the *Gîta* states that he himself is action and asks Arjuna what would become of the world if he ceased to act. The ancient insistence on acquisition of wealth and enjoyment of pleasure, as goals of life which are as important as righteous behaviour and liberation from bodily existence, is now back in Indian philosophical perspective. Though every Indian philosopher would swear by the name of Sri Sankaracharya, few will stop at saying that the world is a pure *mâyâ*, illusion. That the world is *mâyâ* means only that it is relatively real. Most thinkers like S. Radhakrishnan and Rabindranath Tagore have assumed a good measure of Ramanuja's world view into their philosophy.

Karma Samsâra is no longer a fatalistic view of life. It only means that what we are in the present is caused by what we were in the past. But this does not mean that we are not free to fashion our future, nor even unable to change the present itself through our free action.

Secular Values and Secularization : The modern movement in the West towards a secular city and a Death-of-God-theology is not in the least bound to produce a shock in the Hindu mind. Indeed, as Tagore complains, 'the ideal which India tried to realize led her best men to the isolation of a contemplative life' and her penetrating insights into the mysteries of Reality cost her dear in material progress.[14] On the other hand, material success and worldly progress were the ideals of a good section of India's philosophical tradition. There exists a wealth of Hindu literature for the moderns to draw support from, like the *Arthasatra* of Kautilya, the *Pancatantra*, the *Hitopadesa*, the *Kathasaritsagara*, and others which dwell exclusively on worldly success.

Hindu society, having placed power in the hands of kings and assigned spiritual authority to the priests, was never too sacralized to need any radical secularization. Even today, the priests do not command popular respect among the Hindus as they do among Christians and Buddhists. A tradition which did not place a bearded God on a golden throne 'up there' to preside over the affairs of men has nothing to fear about the dethronement of such a God; for it, the denial of all conceivable divinities is the emphatic affirmation of the One Absolute Reality, the One without a second.

Thus, contemporary Hinduism has moved away from its traditional stance to a position where all the dominant values of modern society, both Eastern and Western, are emphatically affirmed.

DIALOGICAL CHRISTIANITY

While these changes were taking place in Hinduism through its encounter with Western Christianity, Christianity itself has felt the urgent need of an open dialogue with the East. We can say that this move began as soon as the Persian translation of the Upanishads of Dara Shikoh was translated into French. Schopenhauer's thought was deeply influenced by the Oriental fragments that reached his hands. So was the thought of many a Western scholar after him.

Comparison of Religions : Scholars were the first to become interested in a deep and thorough study of Hinduism, not in any

---

[14] *Sadhana—The Realization of Life*, p. 4.

popular form, but in its authentic scriptures. According to Max Müller, who dedicated the greater part of his life to the study of Hindu tradition, 'truth' was to be found in the most universal essence of religion and not in its particular manifestations. Though he tried to apply a strictly scientific method to this study and endeavoured to exclude theology and philosophy from its confines, his 'science' of religion ended up as a philosophy of religion. He was followed in this philosophical pursuit by Paul Deussen, Lionel David Barnett and a good many others.

Grammarians and lexicographers like Bötlink, Whitney, Monier Williams, Lannmann and Louis Renou gave a linguistic twist to the study of Hindu scriptures. These philosophical and philological stages were followed by a positivist phase, presided over by sociologists and anthropologists. They tried to present oriental religions as mere expressions of the human spirit spread out in space and time.[15]

Asian scholars, like Radhakrishnan, Zuzuki and Swami Vivekananda, countered this positivist approach with the view that religion is not a creed or code but an insight into reality, the life of the inner spirit available anywhere and everywhere, and that religious truth is the sum total of all religions of this world.

This stand occasioned a rethinking among Western scholars. They were unanimous in stating, against the Asians, that religion is not the sum total of all religions, though 'religion' as a universal religious approach underlies all religions. Each religion is a particular expression of a universal mode of human reaction to Ultimate Reality. Hence, the emphasis should be on what each religion specifically contributed to this universal mode. This must be determined by the historical study of each tradition, helped by theological interpretation and the aid of all other subjects, like philosophy, anthropology, sociology, pyschology and archaeology, dealing with the human phenomenon. This unique character of each religion cannot be grasped by a merely theoretical examination from the outside, but demands an intimate and personal dialogue with those who derive inspiration and spiritual guidance from that religion.

Christian Approach to Non-Christian Religions : Earlier Christian attempts at dialogue with non-Christian religions were clumsy and fruitless, because Christian scholars proceeded to apply their

---

[15] Henri de Lubac, *La Rencontre du Buddhisme et de l'occident*, pp. 262–8.

own theory of religion, derived from Christianity and other Western religions, to the Asian religions, and to judge the latter according to that yardstick.

Thus, Henrick Kraemer, in spite of his sympathy for the East, found a radical opposition between the Biblical religion and the 'natural' religions of the East. The Bible proclaimed the God and Father of Our Lord Jesus Christ who yearns for relation with men, while the Ultimate of natural religions is relationless, actionless, blissful pure essence. For these, the world is a gorgeous yet nauseating pageant, a fascinating yet disgusting process of life, ultimately unreal. These religions are syncretistic, pragmatist, relativist and subjectivist, ending up in an elastic monism. Hence, only through a destructive transformation can they lead to Christ: 'Surrender to Christ, belief in him and allegiance to the prophetic religion of Biblical realism mean, in the first place, a revolution, a total rupture with one's religious past, because it presupposes conversion in the deepest sense of the word.'[16]

J. N. Farquhar, in *The Crown of Hinduism*,[17] admitted the fundamental unity in all religions, based on the sameness of the human heart and mind everywhere. He acknowledged the great good done by all religions, and stated that man can reach God only in utter sincerity and frank acceptance of truth, wherever he finds it. But he maintained the superiority of the Christian position whenever there was a difference of opinion among religions. He also claimed that Christianity alone could survive the modern age which challenges every religious belief and breaks every custom and tradition. 'The needs of the new age, so far as we can see, can be met only by Christianity. Not in arrogance, not in partisanship, do we say this, but with wide open eyes and with full consciousness of the stupendous character of the claim we make.'

On the other hand, William Ernest Hocking saw a certain smooth continuity between the World Religions and Christianity. All men have a common knowledge of God, and not a mere vague spiritual sense. 'The deep naturalness of Christianity' bridges the gap with other religions. It starts by recognizing the sinfulness of man. Precisely on account of the 'God-nature within them' spoken of by the Vedantins, men have to acknowledge themselves as sinners, too. In this, Christianity and World Religions do agree. 'It is through

---

[16] *The Christian Message in a Non-Christian World*, p. 210.
[17] *The Crown of Hinduism* (Oxford, 1913), pp. 31–3.

its dwelling on sin that Christianity for the first time does full honour to human nature.' The natural faith in the beyond, found in all religions, becomes, in Christianity, 'the Fatherhood of God perceived in experience'.[18]

Christianity is Christ, but the Divine Revelation through the creative Logos is neither limited to the history of Israel and the Church, nor totally incomprehensible outside Christian scriptures and tradition. Hocking admitted that even Revelation in Christ would be incomplete until we understand that God in Christ had become incarnate in the whole world. 'The meaning of individual experience tends to unfold in a continuing community of witness-bearers.'[19] Thus Hocking called for a reconception of Christianity itself. 'Since the substance of the Christian faith is given in a perception available to "any man" in his own context and time, an element of universality is built into its nature.'[20] 'The faith of the Christian is contiguous with the nature-faith by which all men live.'[21] Thus, Hocking made very clear what the Christian task in India is : to make this already-existing continuity between the Revelation in Christ and the Hindu experience clear and fully explicit.

VATICAN II AND NON-CHRISTIANS

The Second Vatican Council, which can be called the greatest Christian event of recent times, seems to have endorsed the ecumenism of Hocking on many points and has even gone beyond his restrictions in several of its official documents.

First of all, it recognizes that non-Christian religions, too, are religions in the proper sense of the term and therefore an integral part of humanity's universal response to the call of God. 'Men look to various religions for answers to those profound mysteries of the human condition which today, even as in olden times, deeply stir the human heart.'[22] According to the Council there is a certain basic agreement among these religions. They all recognize 'a certain

[18] William Ernest Hocking, *The Coming World Civilization* (New York: Harper Bros., 1956), pp. 101–7.
[19] *Ibid.,* Cf. Leroy S. Rouner, 'Hocking and India', *Bangalore Theological Forum* (1967), 1, pp. 1–16.
[20] William Ernest Hocking, *op. cit.,* p. 112.
[21] *Ibid.,* p. 113.
[22] *Declaration on the Non-Christian Religions,* n. 1.

perception of that hidden power which hovers over the course of things and over the events of human life', as well as the unity of the human race and of the final goal of man.[23] Furthermore, each one of them has made a unique contribution to the total religious experience of humanity. In this context, Hinduism is specially mentioned for its sense of the mystery and the loving and trusting movement towards God in meditation. All that is 'true and holy' in these World Religions are 'a ray of that truth that enlightens all men'. As the herald of salvation for all men, the Church also has to acknowledge the salvific will of God in 'those who, in shadows and images, seek the unknown God'[24] and respect and foster 'whatever good lies latent in the religious practices and cultures of diverse peoples',[25] for, in Christ, all things are restored and given a new meaning.

In the matter of religious tolerance, the basic fact is the freedom of the individual, which is 'an exceptional sign of the divine image within man'.[26] Truth cannot be imposed on anyone, but by its own light 'makes its entrance into the mind, at once quietly and with power'. Only in and through the exercise of this freedom can true faith gain entrance into the minds of men. 'Of its very nature, the exercise of religion consists, before all else, in those internal, voluntary and free acts whereby man sets the course of his life directly towards God.'[27]

This religious freedom of man, which is based on his unique personality, also gives religion a certain inviolable entity of its own. The social nature of man requires that he should give expression to his internal religious acts in community—in association with others. As the religious acts are superior to man's temporal concerns, so also these social expressions of religion which direct men's lives to God 'transcend by their very nature the order of terrestrial and temporal affairs'.[28] A Government that tampered with them would exceed the limits of its scope and power.

The Church, by its very nature, is a message for all men. The central fact of this Christian message is Christ himself, and the redemption of humanity accomplished through him. This Gospel

23 *Ibid.*, nn. 1 and 2.
24 *Dogmatic Constitution on the Church*, n. 16.
25 *Declaration on Religious Freedom*, n. 1.
26 *Ibid.*
27 *Ibid.*, n. 3.
28 *Ibid.*, nn. 3 and 4.

of salvation was made concrete in the Gospels, written first in view of particular churches. But Christ and his redemption are not the exclusive privilege of any one, but the common right of all men. Hence, that the Gospel be appropriately and adequately announced to all men is not anybody's choice, but the right of all men and the bounden duty of the Christian community which has already received the message. To be communicated appropriately, this Gospel of Christ has, in a way, to become incarnate in every country according to its idioms and thought patterns.

TOWARDS AN INDIAN THEOLOGY

This task of Christianity to become incarnate in the Indian cultural tradition was long recognized. Bhavani Charan Banerjee, a Bengalee Brahmin, born on 11 February, 1861, who, on his conversion to Christianity, took the name of Brahmabandhab Upadhyaya, endeavoured for the whole of his life to spell out the Christian message according to the thought-forms of Sankara's *Advaita* philosophy. Before his conversion, he was a faithful follower of Keshab Chandra Sen's New Dispensation, but since Keshab, Pratap Chundur Mazumdar and other Brahmo leaders stopped short by taking Jesus Christ as a mere man, though a great teacher and social reformer, Upadhyaya had to break with the Brahmos and embrace Christianity at the moment when he realized that Jesus Christ was truly God. For Upadhyaya, Christ fulfilled the universal desire of the Hindus for a sinless Guru (*Sat Guru, Nishkalakâvatâr*). According to him, Jesus of Nazareth, truly the unique Son of God and glorified in his terrestrial existence through the resurrection, was for all human history a focal point in which man could concentrate all his dissipated powers and attain the Absolute in the one Word. All religions converged towards this one ideal Guru. The reconciliation between Christianity and Hinduism could be achieved only in this one Teacher. 'Let us be called by any name. We mean to preach the reconciliation of all religions in Christ whom we believe to be perfectly divine and perfectly human.'[29]

In Jesus of Nazareth, who was at the same time truly the Son of God and the son of man in one single personality, the two irreconcilables in identity—namely, the *nirguna* and *saguna*

[29] B. Animananda, *The Blade, Life and Work of Brahmabandhah Upadhyaya* (Calcutta: Roy & Son).

views of reality—are reconciled. He is, on the one hand, the Absolute, and, at the same time, unifies and summarizes in himself all the phenomenal world.

In Brahmabandhab's view, the *Avatârs* of Hinduism, and especially Sri Krishna, do not conflict with the one Incarnation of God in Jesus Christ. The *Avatârs* only present and focalize the cultural and religious feelings and aspirations of India. The pranks of child Sri Krishna are just the playful expressions of an innocent child which, in the Hindu tradition, symbolize the meaning of creation as the *lîla*, or play of God.

In this harmonious experience of Christian faith and Hindu tradition, Brahmabandhab became the most ardent fighter for India's freedom from British rule, but lack of understanding and co-operation on the part of Christian authorities was the biggest stumbling block in the way of Brahmabandhab's endeavours for creating an Indian Christian theology.

Call of God in the Heart: If Brahmabandhab tried to centre an Indian theology around the tension between the one Incarnation of the Son of God in Jesus of Nazareth and the many *Avatârs* of India, another Hindu convert, Sri Vengal Chakkarai, tried to focus it on the interior call of God. According to him, purely theoretical comparisons between Hinduism and Christianity do not help to convince anyone. The beginning should be made from the centre of human experience. Paul and Augustine, and every other convert to Christ's Gospel, answered Christ's call within their own hearts. 'To this extent, the Indian maxim that each religion is good to its own followers is right. It is right, up to the stage when a new element enters which shifts the centre of gravity from the old to the new.'[30]

Christianity is 'not a different religion so much as a different region'. No one actually prefers it to any other 'till the Lord chooses to call him'. 'There is nothing in Christianity that can validate its contents, except the call and election of God.'[31] This is not to deny the need for teaching and preaching, but only to emphasize the pre-eminent importance of the internal experience of the Son of God in the heart of each individual. Salvation in Christ is a call made to every man.

[30] Quoted by P. T. Thomas in *The Theology of Chakkarai* (Madras: C.L.S., 1967), p. 126.
[31] *Ibid.*, pp. 126–7.

Gospel and India : Even in reflexion on the Gospels, the Indian outlook should be taken into account. The whole life of Christ, his words and deeds, should be presented against the basic outlook of *Karma* and *Dharma*, action and righteousness, which are the bases of Hindu spiritual outlook. Here, it is not a question of the substance of the Christian message, but of the manner in which one receives the message, the points of emphasis which should correspond to the mode of thought and aspirations of the people in India today.

Thus the best way of presenting Christ is not an abstract discussion of the hypostatic union, which sounds very much like a metaphysical struggle between divine existence and human nature, a mystery to be blindly accepted and believed in. His is the ideal manhood to which every man has to conform. His uniqueness should be pointed out, especially in his life of prayer and sinlessness.

Similarly, his miracles should not simply be looked upon as extraordinary phenomena, purely intended for exciting wonder. They are the expressions of his *karma*, saving action for the sake of the suffering humanity. They were not totally unrelated to the people before whom they were worked. They were Christ's answer to the earnest petitions of the people : in them the force of Christ's personality and the faith of the sufferer work together. Christ himself labours and in a way suffers in them and shows his concern for the people, and so symbolizes the work of the suffering creator, reminiscent of the creative *yajna* of Prajapati in Hindu mythology. This creative sacrifice culminates on the cross in the redemptive death of Christ, which ushers in a new *Sakti*, the redemptive power. In a way, the miracles are the manifestation of the heavenly kingdom, the Vaikuntha, in the world of time.

Thus, every phase of Christ's life, work and message has a particular side which appeals to the Indian mentality and answers to the yearnings of the Indian heart. The function of an Indian theology is to reveal these points of emphasis.

Conclusion

The encounter between Hinduism and Christianity has brought about salutary changes in both the religious traditions; in a way, their preoccupations and interests seem to converge to a common point.

(1) There is a certain convergence with regard to the value of this material world. Christ is the Son of God, sent by the Father to reintegrate all things under his leadership, to give meaning, unity and direction to this dissipated world. Hinduism is struggling today to give this world its proper meaning—subordinate to the spiritual, but with proper accent placed on the need for economic growth and on the urgency to satisfy the material needs of the suffering masses.

(2) There is convergence in the understanding of the Word of Divine Revelation. For Christianity, Christ is the Word of God announced by the Prophets and made manifest in the flesh in the fullness of time to transform the whole world into a willing response to the Father. For Hinduism, too, the primary concern is that the *Sabda*, the Word, handed down by the *Rishis*, may be realized by the Indian masses in their personal realization and daily activity.

(3) Christianity believes in the one Incarnation of God, accomplished in Jesus of Nazareth, who was raised from the dead and made Lord and Saviour. The Indian concept of *avatârs*, too, proceeds through the prior forms of Fish, Tortoise, Boar, Man-Lion, and so on, towards the culmination of divine manifestation in Sri Krishna, the ideal of *dharma*, and the final *avatâr, Kalki*, who will be the fulfilment of justice.

(4) Both Hinduism and Christianity have arrived at a new spirit of tolerance for all religions. This is not a matter of mere convenience or of accommodation to circumstances, but the conclusion of theological thought.

(5) To both of them, sectarian or merely nationalistic considerations seem to contradict the very spirit of religion. Both are forced to take into view the whole human race as a single family, and to propose the message of salvation only while considering the whole human life in all time and in all places.

These converging aspects of religious thought demonstrate only one form of the converging preoccupations and aspirations of the human spirit today.

CHAPTER XIV
EPILOGUE

This book has attempted to describe the interaction that took place between the various thought-patterns, cultural trends and religious systems which met together on the Indian sub-continent, and helped to form a single and yet diversified Indian tradition. In the meeting between the Indus Valley civilization and the Aryan nomadic culture, two main world traditions fused together to create a balanced view of human life and ideals. While the Aryan strand emphasized the spiritual aspirations of man's nobler qualities and the heavenly gods, most of whom rode on horseback, the pre-Aryan line gave special emphasis to the bodily side of human life, with fertility cults, the horned god sitting in the midst of animals, together with the ideal of life-long asceticism which means the sublimation of this earth.

Jainism and Buddhism indicated the re-emergence of pre-Aryan and religious values and attitudes and they were able to rule India for over a millennium, but in the end, Hinduism absorbed and made its own all their positive emphases, to such an extent as to make them seem to be mere heresies of Hinduism. They were almost eradicated from India as independent entities. However, it should be remembered that the dominant values of post-Vedic Hinduism are the generous bequest of their ancient traditions.

The encounter between post-Vedic Hinduism and the Dravidian tradition was so smooth and spontaneous that it is very difficult to discern any specific Dravidian contributions to the common pool with any semblance of exactitude. However, the Dravidian tradition can still boast that Tamil survived Sanskrit as a living language, and that southern identity was kept intact in manners and customs. Similarly, the pre-Aryan tribal traditions have kept themselves alive through long centuries of Brahmanization and Sanskritization and have preserved their identity almost intact,

151

though their relationship with the *one* Indian historical tradition remains somewhat ambiguous.

The Hindu-Muslim encounter was a happy one in the beginning, but with the ensuing political conflict the two religious traditions drifted far apart and became rigid in their mutual antagonism. This opposing polarity fixed their roles in the formation of the one historic entity of India's past.

On the other hand, the encounter between Hinduism and Western Christianity was not a happy one for a long time, owing to the tension created by the political aspirations of the Western Powers. Today, however, in a world reduced in size by the facility of global communications, the two great religious traditions of East and West are drawing closer to a common position on several points. An active and productive dialogue between the two traditions has yet to begin, and what exists at present are, at best, two monologues which pass each other at a tangent.

Since Christianity has a worldwide diffusion, it is conscious of religious pluralism in the world. It has become suddenly aware that, even with the largest following in the so-called developed countries, it is only one among World Religions, and serves only about one-fifth of the human race. It has also become actually conscious of the radical difference in thought-forms, idioms and cultural expressions between East and West. Hence, Christianity feels the urgent need for dialogue with other religions. Unfortunately, Christianity has now been stuck in the Graeco-Judaic thought-pattern for centuries, and has very little familiarity with the soul of Asia where flourish the great Eastern religions—Buddhism, Hinduism and Confucianism. Only when Christianity has fully expressed its religious message in an Eastern religious idiom and imagery can it start a meaningful conversation with the East.

Hinduism, Buddhism and Confucianism, owing to their narrow geographical concentrations, do not feel a serious need for dialogue. Though they have moved into the twentieth century and have radically altered their attitudes to modern secular problems, they have done this rather unconsciously. With regard to religion and culture, they feel secure in their geographical confines, and are living mostly on their ancestral patrimony with very little effort to invest it in the modern century. But the present communications explosion is pushing them into the middle of the nuclear age and they will soon feel their involvement in the problems of the day.

Only such an involvement can force them to rethink and reformulate their religious and cultural values in the modern idiom. Only then will a significant dialogue with the West come into being.

The geographically intermediate world of the Muslims appears the most insecure in this East-West encounter. Having close ties with both East and West, the Muslims are in the most advantageous position to initiate, maintain and direct such a dialogue. But the Muslim world carries a huge backlog of sad memories, both from Europe and from India. In Europe, it lost its influence and prestige long ago. The Hindu-Muslim conflict on the Indian sub-continent is too recent to permit any open and whole-hearted dialogue.

Perhaps the way out of this impasse in dialogue is provided by the rapidity with which the world is moving ahead. Scientific and technological progress is posing problems which seem to threaten the whole human race. The imminent prospect of Atom-Bacteria-Chemical warfare, which may mean the destruction of a good section of humanity, should shift the centre of dialogue from metaphysics and questions of belief to the secular problems that affect human existence itself. Perhaps this is where religion should rightly belong; human hearts will draw closer when men discuss, not their differences and past grievances, but their common problems and common tasks towards building up a future which does not discriminate between East and West.

BIBLIOGRAPHY

Abbot, John, *The Keys of Power, A Study of Indian Ritual and Belief* (New York: E. P. Dutton & Co., 1932).

Acharya, Prasanna Kumar, *Glories of India, On Indian Culture and Civilization* (Allahabad, 1952).

Alberuni's India, An account of the Religion, Philosophy, Literature, Geography, Chronology, Astronomy, Customs, Laws and Astrology of India about A.D. 1030, ed. Edward C. Sachau (Delhi: S. Chand & Co., 1st Indian reprint, 1964).

Apte, V. M., *Social and Religious Life in the Grihya Sûtras,* with a Foreword by R. D. Karmarkar (Ahmedabad, 1939).

Atkins, Samuel D., *Pushan in the Rig Veda* (Princeton, 1941).

Banergee, Indubhusan, *Evolution of the Khalsa,* Vol. I, The Foundation of the Sikh Panth (Calcutta, 1936).

Banerjee, Gauranga Nath, *Hellenism in Ancient India* (Calcutta, 1920).

Basham, A. L., *The Wonder that was India* (London, 1961).

Bhandarkar, D. R., *Some Aspects of Ancient Indian Culture,* Sir William Meyer Lectures, 1938–9 (Madras University, 1940).

Bhartrihari: Poems, trs. Barbara Stoler Mitler (New York: Columbia University Press, 1967).

Brown, W. Norman. 'The Beginnings of Civilization in India', *Journal of the American Oriental Society,* 59 (1939), 32–44.

Brown, W. Norman, *Man in the Universe, Some Cultural Continuities in India* (Berkeley and Los Angeles: University of California Press, 1966).

Byron, Robert, *An Essay on India* (London: George Routledge, 1931).

Campbell, Alexander, *The Heart of India* (New York, Alfred A. Knoff, 1958).

Chand, Tara, *Influence of Islam on Indian Culture* (Allahabad: Indian Press, 1946).

Chaudhury, Makhan Lal Roy, *The DIN-I-ILAHI or the Religion of Akbar* (Calcutta: Dasgupta & Co., 2nd ed., 1952).

Court, Maj. Henry, *History of the Sikhs* or translation of the Sikkhan de Raj de Vikhia (Lahorefi, 1888; 2nd imp., Calcutta, 1959).

Das, Abinas Chandra, *Rig Vedic Culture* (Calcutta: R. Cambray & Co., 1925).

Deb, Harit Krishna, 'Vedic India and the Middle East', *Journal of the Royal Asiatic Society of Bengal,* 13 (1947), 121–43.

Dumont, Louis, 'The Functional Equivalents of the Individual in Caste Society', *Contributions to Indian Sociology,* VIII, 85–99.

Dutt, Romesh C., *Early Hindu Civilization, 2000 B.C.–A.D. 320* (Calcutta: R. P. Mitra, 1927).

Emerson, Gertrude, *Voiceless India* (New York: John Day, 1930; revised ed., 1944).

Field, Dorothy, *The Religion of the Sikhs* (London: John Murray, 1914).

Gibb, H. A. R., *Mohamedanism, An Historical Survey* (New York: Oxford University Press, 1962).

155

Gonda, J., *Epithets in the Rig Veda* ('s-Gravenhage: Mouton & Co., 1959).
Gonda, J., *Aspects of Early Vishnuism* (Utrecht: N. V. A. Oosthoek's uitgevers Mij, 1954).
Gonda, J., *Four Studies in the Language of the Veda* ('s-Gravenhage: Mouton & Co., 1959).
Hartog, P. J., 'The Indian Universities', *India*, ed. D. R. Bhandarkar (Calcutta, 1929), 138–50.
Heimann, Betty, 'Contrasts in Fundamental Postulates: Monotheism or Henotheism? Miracles or Laws of Nature? History or Mythology?' *Dr S. K. Belvalkar Felicitation Volume* (Banaras: Motilal Banarsidass, 1957), 219–27.
Husain, Abid S., *The National Culture of India*, revised and enlarged 2nd ed. (London: Asia Publishing House, 1961).
Husain, Yusuf, *Glimpses of Mediaeval Indian Culture* (Bombay: Asia Publishing House, 2nd ed., 1959).
Ikram, S. M., *Muslim Civilization in India* (New York: Columbia University Press, 1964).
Ishwaran, K., *Shivapur, a South Indian Village* (London: Routledge & Kegan Paul, 1968).
Jairazbhoy, R. A., *Foreign Influence in Ancient India* (New York: Asia Publishing House, 1963).
Jarries, Pierre du, S.J., *Akbar and the Jesuits*, trs. C. H. Payne (London: George Routledge & Sons, 1926).
Keay, F. E., *Kahir and his Followers* (Calcutta: Association Press, 1931).
Kohli, Surindar Singh, *A Critical Study of Adi Granth* (New Delhi: The Punjab Writers' Co-operative Industrial Society, 1961).
Kulkarni, Chidambra, *Ancient Indian History and Culture* (Bombay: Kartanak Publishing House, 3rd imp., 1966).
Kumarappa, Bharatan, *The Hindu Conception of the Deity as culminating in Ramanuja*, with a Foreword by Dr L. D. Barnett (London: Luzac & Co., 1934).
Latif, Syed Abdul, *An Outline of the Cultural History of India* (Hyderabad: The Institute of Indo-Middle East Cultural Studies, 1958).
Levi, Sylvain, 'La Transmigration des Ames dans les Croyances Hindu', *Conférences au Musée Guimet*, 1903–4 (Paris, 1904).
Lytton, V. A. G. R., 'Hindu-Muslim Unity', *India*, ed. R. D. Bhandarkar (Calcutta, 1929), 175–80.
Macauliffe, Max Arthur, *The Sikh Religion, Its Gurus, Sacred Writings and Authors* (Oxford: Clarendon Press, 1909). (6 Vols.)
Majd Majdud Sanai Abu L. of Ghanza, *The First Book of the Madiqatu 'l-Haqiqat, or the Enclosed Garden of Truth*, trs. Maj. J. Stephenson (Calcutta, 1910).
Majumdar, R. C., *Ancient India* (Banaras: Motilal Banarsidass, 1952).
Majundar, S. K., *Jinnah and Gandhi* (Calcutta: Firma K. L. Mukhopadhyay, 1966).
Mehta, G. L., *Understanding India* (London: Asia Publishing House, 1959).
Mélanges sur l'Inde, Vol. I, Cahiers du Sud, June-July, 1941.
Modak, Manorama R., *The Land and the People of India* (Philadelphia and New York: J. B. Lippincott Co., revised ed., 7th printing, 1960).
Morgan, Kenneth W., ed., *The Religion of the Hindus* (New York: The Ronald Press Co., 1953).
Narang, Sir Gokul Chand, *Transformation of Sikhism* (Lahore, 3rd ed., 1946). (2 vols.)

Nizami, Khaliq Ahamad, *Some Aspects of Religion and Politics in India during the 13th Century* (Asia Publishing for Aligarh Muslim University, 1961).

Pinch, Trevor, *Stark India* (London: Hutchinson & Co., 1930).

Pincott, Frederic, *Sikhism in its Relation to Mohammadanism* (London: W. H. Allen & Co., 1885).

Potter, Karl H., *Presuppositions of India's Philosophies* (Englewood Cliffs, New Jersey: Prentice-Hall).

Prasad, Jwala, *Indian Epistemology* (Lahore: Moltilal Banarsidass, 1939).

Puri, Baij Nath, *India as described by early Greek writers* (Allahabad: The Indian Press, 1939).

Pym, Michael, *The Power of India* (London: G. P. Putnam's Sons, 1930).

Qasem, M. A., *Muslim Rule in India* (Bagherat: Khulna, 1956).

Quereshi, Ishtiaq Husain, *The Administration of the Sultanate of Delhi* (Lahore: Sh. Muhammad Ashraf, 2nd ed., 1944).

Rai, Lajpat, *Unhappy India* (Calcutta: Banna Publishing Co., 1928).

Rajvade, V. K., 'Words in Rig Veda', *Bhandarkar Oriental Research Institute, Poona, Annals*, 9 (1928), 25–32; 183–266.

Ranga Iyer, C. S., *Father India, A Reply to Mother India* (London: Selwyn & Blount, 1927).

Sell, Canon, *Studies in Islam* (Madras, 1928).

Shamasashtri, R., 'Dravidian Culture', *Bhandarkar Oriental Research Institute, Poona, Annals*, 11 (1930), 336–60.

Shelat, J. M., *Akbar*, Vols. I and II (Bombay: Bharatiya Vidya Bhavan, 1959).

Sinder, Leon, *Caste Instability in Moghul India* (Seoul, Korea: International Culture Research Centre, 1964).

Sirkar, Benoy Kumar, *The Political Institutions and Theories of the Hindus, A Study in Comparative Politics* (Leipzig: Verlag von Markett & Pelters, 1922).

Srinivasachari, P. N., *Ramanuja's Idea of the Finite Self*, with a Foreword by S. Kuppuswami Sastri (Madras: Longmans, Green & Co., 1928).

Tilak, Bal Gangadhar, *The Arctic Home in the Vedas* (Poona: Tilak Bros., 1925).

Tilak, Bal Gangadhar, *The Orion or Researches into the Antiquity of the Vedas* (Poona: Tilak Bros., 4th ed., 1955).

Tilak, Bal Gangadhar, 'Chaldean and Indian Vedas', *Sir R. G. Bhandarkar Commemorative Essays* (Poona: Bhandarkar Oriental Research Institute, 1917).

Valiuddin, Mir, *The Quranic Sufism* (Delhi: Motilal Banarsidass, 1959).

Venkata, Romanan K., *Nagarjuna's Philosophy as presented in the Maha Prajnaparamita Sastra* (Rutland, Vermont: Charles E. Tuttle Co., for the Harvard-Yenching Institute, 1966).

Weber, Max, *The Religion of India; The Sociology of Hinduism and Buddhism*, trs. Hans H. Gerth and Don Martindale (Glencoe, Illinois: The Free Press, 1958).

Whitney, William D., 'On the History of the Vedic Texts', *Journal of the American Oriental Society*, 4 (1854), 247–62.

Wood, Ernest, *Great Systems of Yoga* (New York: The Citadel Press, Paperback, 1966).

Transliterations used in this book

ā or ã as â
ḍ as dh
ī as î
ḷ as l
ṃ or ṁ as m
ñ as jn
ṅ as ng
ṇ as n
ō as ô
ṛ as ri
ṣ as sh
ś as s
ṭ as th
ū as û

INDEX

Index prepared by Brenda Hall, M.A., Registered Indexer of the Society of Indexers.